Living Successfully in a Dangerous World

Studies in 1 Peter

Stephen Gaukroger

Christian Focus

For details of our titles visit us on our web site
http://www.geanies.org.uk/cfp

© Stephen Gaukroger

ISBN 1 85792 393 6

Published in 1998
by Christian Focus Publications
Geanies House, Fearn, Ross-shire,
IV20 1TW, Great Britain

Cover design by Donna Macleod

Contents

Also published by Christian Focus

BATTLEGROUND

*Joshua's Strategies for Leadership
and Spiritual Warfare*

The Book of Joshua details how Joshua led the
people of God to inherit the Promised Land. In
doing so, he displayed various leadership qualities
that are essential characteristics of all who are
gifted to lead God's people. Stephen Gaukroger
examines these features and applies them to
common situations that local church leaders will
find themselves in today.

But the Book of Joshua is not just about
Joshua's leadership capabilities. The book also
describes how all the people of God were involved
in the warfare that was required to capture the
Promised Land from their enemies. In the accounts
of their victories and set-backs, we are given
principles for us as Christians to use in spiritual
warfare today.

ISBN 185792 163 1   *176 pages*

Stephen Gaukroger is the pastor of Gold Hill
Baptist Church in Chalfont St. Peter,
Buckinghamshire, England.

Introduction

No one is absolutely certain when 1 Peter was written, although it seems that it was written about thirty years after the death of Jesus. The reason for this conclusion is that it is likely that Peter was martyred in the Nero Persecution in the 60s. So in this letter Peter is writing to a struggling people to tell them that knowing God and following him will make a difference in their lives and will cause them to live successfully in a dangerous world.

Peter, along with James and John, was one of the inner circle whom Jesus chose to be with him on special occasions such as the Transfiguration and the raising of Jairus' daughter from death, as well as his agony in Gethsemane. Yet Peter was not a superhuman character – he knew what it was to live in an ordinary world and make lots of errors. He had an amazing propensity for inappropriate comment. Lots of times in bubbling nervousness he would say the wrong thing. And he would go down in history as the one who denied Jesus. Yet although he was a giant with clay feet, God used him to help us by writing this letter about living successfully in this world.

The letter was sent from Peter to a scattered community of people living in what is modern day Turkey. The places are listed in route order indicating it is a circular letter, perhaps dictated to Silas (5:12). As a courier takes Peter's letters he stops of at Pontus and then Galatia and so on.

> Peter, an apostle of Jesus Christ,
>
> To God's elect, strangers in the world, scattered throughout Pontus, Galatia, Cappadocia, Asia and Bithynia, who have been chosen according to the foreknowledge of God the Father, through the sanctifying work of the Spirit, for obedience to Jesus Christ and sprinkling by his blood:
>
> Grace and peace be yours in abundance (1:1-2).

Authority of Christ

What does Peter mean when he writes that he was an *apostle*? He is indicating that he was sent by Jesus Christ who himself was sent by God. That is what the term 'Christ' means. Peter's claim to fame is that his ambassadorial status comes from being sent by Jesus Christ, the saviour of the world. That is very impressive. Ambassadors of countries have a certain status, not because of anything in themselves but because of who they represent. Peter is saying, 'What I am about to say to you has status, importance, vitality and power because I represent the greatest authority in the world.' Peter is an apostle of Jesus Christ and we must allow the wonder of that statement to impact us. This letter comes to us from one who represents the anointed, sent Saviour.

In the late 1990s there is a global obsession with power. Who is in control in the world? Do the G7 nations determine the fate of the planet economically? Does the United Nations determine the fate of the planet politically? Who has the power in a world gone wrong? I only have confidence in the act of preaching because I believe that God is still on the throne, and that the destiny of our planet does not rest with the G7 Nations or with the United Nations or with any single government leader or philosophical viewpoint. Therefore, our message is not outdated. As we stand on the verge of a new millennium we re-assure ourselves that the power of the universe still rests in the hands of God. The One who sent Peter sends us. The One who equipped Peter equips us. The One who was Lord of the first century is Lord of the twentieth century and will be Lord of the twenty-first century as well.

We own the name of Jesus Christ. Names in the Bible mean different things, unlike western culture where names don't say anything about our characters. But in the Bible names are very important indeed. Peter is not using 'Jesus Christ' as a kind of throwaway line. This name is a determination of authority, hence when we pray we pray in the name of Jesus. Of course there is nothing magical about the name of Jesus; it's not the name, it's the power behind the name, the power of Jesus Christ. We are sent by the One who has all power in his control. So be encouraged, we are followers of the greatest One who has ever lived. There will never be a greater name than the name of Jesus.

Christians are significant
In the Old Testament the Israelites are described as the chosen people of God, set apart to him. Sadly they often had a wrong understanding what 'chosen' meant. They often thought they were chosen because they were better than the Gentile nations. Throughout their history, God found ways of making them understand that they were chosen to *serve*. In particular, they were chosen to be a light to the Gentiles, to be a vehicle through which God's power could flow and bless the nations. God's purpose was fulfilled ultimately in the coming of Jesus Christ. Now both Gentiles and Jews through Jesus Christ are part of the chosen ones, those who have been given special status – not for pride but for service.

There is a tremendous wonder in being chosen by God. Many of you will remember, from many situations, the pain of not being chosen. Some of you are feeling valueless, feeling that nobody does value you; no-one would choose you given a choice. Deep inside you feel unworthy, uncared for and unlovely because you don't feel loved and cared for. Life can be a lonely experience sometimes. Even in the midst of a crowd we can be alone. But to believers God says, 'I cared enough about you to choose you. Nobody else may choose you, but I chose you in Jesus Christ.' God saw all believers before the foundation of the world. And he loved them to the point of sending his Son to die for them.

The biblical doctrine of predestination is complex and difficult. But it is not revealed merely for our intellectual stimulation, nor for Christians to claim that we are better than other people. The great thing is not that we are better but that God has placed his mark of love on our lives. If nobody else seems to care for you, I remind you that you belong to the family of God. God loves you, he chose you and cares for you.

This is true even though you realise you are 'strangers in the world'. The actual phrase in the original language speaks about dislocation, as if we are in a place we don't expect to be. I don't know whether you ever feel this, but I hope you do. If God's Spirit is at work in you, then from time to time you will feel a stranger in the world. Because God's Spirit lives in you, you find yourself in conversations, you find yourself in locations, you find yourself doing things that don't quite fit. That is because day by day God is preparing us on earth for a place where we will never feel dislocated, where we will always feel totally at home.

What a wonderful thrilling thing that is. As

the Negro spiritual says, 'This world is not my home, I am just a passing through.' It is important to remember that. Don't get too comfortable here, you will not be around that long. Prepare for a world where you will be for ever – where you will be no longer a stranger, no longer living successfully in a struggling world but living perfectly in a perfect world. Get ready to receive all God's glory – we are being prepared to worship him as non-dislocated beings perfectly for ever in heaven with God. So get excited about that.

What a perspective this gives with which to regard our fellow believers. We are going to spend eternity with them. That can be quite a shock to the system to remember.

We are dislocated and Peter is quite clear about this. Part of the struggle we have in this difficult world is that we have within us the Holy Spirit and because he has been placed within us, we somehow don't feel as if we fit anymore. In addition to all the normal tensions of living, we feel like strangers in the world because God's Spirit has come to live within us. He is transforming us to be like Jesus Christ, therefore the sinful world system grates against us. It is a struggle.

But it is also a joy because we are recruiting others to be strangers. That is what evangelism is. It is saying to people to prepare for another world, to know God now and to prepare for living then. What a great privilege – we are inviting them to the adventure, not just of a lifetime, but the adventure of eternity when the struggles will one day end. One day every tear will be wiped away. We will spend eternity together, no longer strangers but friends made completely whole.

Christians are sanctified
We see the sense of the security of Christians in three phrases: they were chosen according the to the foreknowledge of God the Father through the sanctifying work of the Spirit for obedience to Jesus Christ. Notice the Trinitarian reference, straight away at the start of this letter. God the Father chooses, the Holy Spirit sanctifies, and it is all that we might be obedient to Jesus.

Although they are all involved in everything, they have different roles. The doctrine of the Trinity is implied throughout scripture but hardly ever explicitly stated, and so is quite difficult for us to understand. Sometimes, illustrations, such as water which has three forms (ice, steam and liquid), or a three legged stool are used. But such explanations are completely inadequate to express the way God operates.

God the Father was involved in choosing us. That is the source of our security – God with all his authority chose us. In doing so he has affirmed us. What a thought, the highest possible power in the universe affirms us.

And he has done it through the sanctifying work of the Holy Spirit, that is, the Holy Spirit makes us holy. The words 'holy' and 'sanctified' are very closely related, they mean 'set apart' – not set apart physically but set apart in a deep inner reality. Holiness in the New Testament is characterised by an inner power to do the right thing. The Holy Spirit comes into our lives to transform us and we are made holy.

Whatever else the Holy Spirit wants to do in our lives, he wants to make us holy. The Holy Spirit cannot come without his holiness, so whatever experiences of the Spirit we claim we must have holiness when he comes. He cannot come in any other form. He longs to be even more at work making us holy. In other words we are in a partnership business in living successfully in a dangerous world. We don't have to grit our teeth and say, 'I am going to live a more holy life.' That's like a new year's resolution with a spiritual veneer. If that is all there is to spiritual holiness most of us are in deep trouble. Our willpower, by itself, falls at the trivial. But the Holy Spirit accompanies us – as we work in the office, as we travel to appointments, as we meet people. So often Satan blinds us to this fact. And sadly we quench the Holy Spirit and he gets less and less influence in our lives.

The Holy Spirit longs to flow into our lives so that we will be obedient to Jesus Christ. The secret of successful living is that the Holy Spirit is working within us to lead us to obey Jesus. He is not working primarily so that we are happy or successful, sometimes these things accompany spiritual life, though not always. We have been called to this great and glorious Christian ministry – to do what Jesus said. Jesus himself was obedient to his Father and we are called to be obedient to Christ.

The church which is compellingly attractive to people who are not Christians is one which is paramountly committed to obedience. When we become committed to obedience to Jesus we become like him – and he is an incredibly attractive figure. The caricature of Jesus that so many of our non-Christian friends and neighbours have is dreadfully off-putting to them in terms of their Christian faith. One of the things I absolutely hate about the media is its image of the clergy. They are inevitably geriatric, bigoted or effeminate or just downright wet. And sadly in a lot of cases it is true. But that is not my understanding of Christian leadership or of Jesus. Jesus threw the money changers out of the Temple, he demanded total allegiance and loyalty. And when we model obedience to this Jesus, we become the attractive community because even though we are saying strong things about sexual morality and about ethical integrity, what we model becomes compulsively attractive. The challenge to us is to submit our sexual lives, our business ethics, every part of what we do, to the Lordship of Christ. Without that obedience we are half-Christian but with that obedience what sounds incredibly restricting is gloriously releasing. What a wonderful thing that is.

1

An Attitude of Praise
(1 Peter 1:3-9)

As he begins his letter Peter points to one of the keys to living successfully in this dangerous world – an attitude of praise. Peter was writing to believers who were facing difficult and dangerous situations. Perhaps we might expect their natural response not to be one of praise. Yet Peter begins by saying: 'Praise be to the God and Father of our Lord Jesus Christ' (1:3). Why? Because praise forces us away from self-analysis into an absorption with God our Father. The more time we spend dwelling on ourselves the bigger our problems become. But when we dwell on the living God our problems assume appropriate proportions. The psalmists knew the truth of this, for we find psalm after psalm absorbed in praise and adoration of the King of Kings.

Peter's opening words, 'Praise be to God', would have been a very common saying in the ancient world, because there were gods of all kinds. Everyone was religious – they all worshipped some god or other. So Peter was at pains to point out that in this pluralistic world it was not just any god that he was worshipping, but the God who is 'the Father of our Lord Jesus Christ'.

This definition of God is one we need to hear more and more today. Our own society is becoming increasingly pluralistic. Religions, cults and philosophies abound and 'god', in some form or other, is worshipped. The widespread recognition of New Age philosophy has made it seem socially acceptable for people to draw on some supernatural force or power outside themselves. But Christians don't simply draw on some power, they draw on a God who is defined by his relationship with his Son. We worship God who is the Father of our Lord Jesus Christ. And if we are in Christ, that means that he is our Father too.

The new birth
God is not Father to every human being, for the Bible describes him as Father of those who are in Christ. So we can only call him Father through faith in his Son. In God's great mercy, he has given us new birth into his family. Being born again is the start to living successfully in a dangerous world.

I became a Christian as a young child, when I prayed a very simple prayer: 'Lord, please give me whatever it is my parents have.' My parents' faith was so strong and influential, that I wanted to be like them and, although I wasn't baptised until the age of fourteen, I know it was as I prayed that prayer that I was born again. Some come to know Jesus in a moment, perhaps at a great crusade or campaign meeting. But many others come to Christ gradually. It is not important to know the date – it is just important to understand the reality of being a believer.

Peter, however, does not merely tell us that God has given us new birth, and then leave it there. No, he goes on to specify three things that are ours through this new birth.

A living hope

Firstly, this new birth gives us 'a living hope through the resurrection of Jesus from the dead' (1:3). In Dante's *Inferno*, he pictures the door of hell as bearing the inscription, 'All hope abandon, ye who enter here.' For many in the ancient world, hopelessness was their condition, for they had no concept of life beyond the grave. Death was the end, which is why every time Paul talked about the resurrection the reaction he got was one of amazement (see Acts 17:31-34).

They certainly didn't have a living hope, but Christians do have a living hope 'through the resurrection of Jesus'. If we are to live successfully in this dangerous world, we must hold firmly to this living hope. There will never be a living hope apart from the hope brought about by the resurrection. All human life comes ultimately to an end. But for believers there is a hope which ends not in death but with a Saviour who holds their hand and takes them into eternity. We have a living hope, because Jesus is alive.

There are religious leaders, intellectuals and philanthropists who have had a profound impact on the human race. But none

> Recently I visited Northern Ireland. The sentiment I heard expressed most often was: 'We don't believe the cease fire will last, but we hope.' But there will never be any hope in the political arena until Jesus Christ is welcomed at the conference table.

of them can provide a living hope, because only Jesus came back from the dead.

Our hope is based not on our own merits but on the fact of the resurrection. Every day we are aware of how alive our hope is. Every day in the heart of the believer is Easter Day. The grave has been ripped apart. Death tried to consume Jesus but after three days he broke his power. He is the only one who could not be defeated by death and hell and Satan. But by his resurrection he defeated Satan and sin and death. We may not see the fruit of that now, but the day is coming when our living hope will be fulfilled.

Have you ever known a time of great blessing and closeness to God interrupted by the devil as he whispers in your ear, 'Don't get too excited, it's not going to last, you will be just as bad in an hour's time.' When the devil reminds you of your past, you remind him of his future. We have a living hope, because Jesus is alive.

A guaranteed inheritance

We are not only given a living hope, we are also given a guaranteed inheritance, one that can never 'perish, spoil or fade' (1:4). To the people who first received this letter, inheritance meant only one thing – it meant the land. The trouble was, however, that people kept stealing the land from them. They would gain a bit, and lose a bit, so it went on throughout the history of the Jews. But Peter reminds them that when you are a Christian you have an inheritance that can never be taken from you. They will have a security far greater than the land which they had always seen as their inheritance.

Peter's language is very homely and practical here. He uses the words 'perish', 'spoil' and 'fade'. These are three of the common ways that possessions can become damaged or devalued over time. But Peter guarantees that in all our struggles we have an inheritance that will never fail for it is 'kept in heaven' for us.

It is interesting that when people come into money they are often not sure what to do with it to keep it safe. Is it best stored in a box under a mattress? Would it be wiser to invest it? Would it be safer in a bank? And so on. We fear theft, we fear a bad investment. But the believer has an inheritance that is kept secure. The Greek word used means to post a sentry at duty. If an army had treasure on camp, the money tent would have armed soldiers placed outside so that the treasure would be kept safe from attack. No-one would be able to steal it. And this is the meaning of Peter's words: not only do we have a living hope based on the resurrection, that nothing can take away, we also have a *guaranteed* inheritance. Inflation cannot destroy it, neither can it be taken from us by some powerful force. Not all our mistakes or worries or feelings can take away this inheritance which God is guarding. It is kept for those who through faith are shielded by his power.

A certain protection
In the first century any number of things could happen to you as a Christian; the worst, of course, was that you would be imprisoned and possibly even martyred by the Roman authorities. But even if you were not subjected to such extreme persecution, there were many other difficulties. There was a kind of guild of merchants from which a person was excluded if he didn't offer incense to the local deity. And there were many other ways in which the Christian was marginalised in day to day life in the ancient world.

However, the Christian is promised not only a living hope and a guaranteed inheritance, but also God's shielding and protection here on earth. We may not be aware of God's protection in our lives, and we may never know on this side of eternity just what we have been protected from, even this week. We are shielded by God, invisibly. Unknown to us, the Lord is seeking out our best interest. Paul, in his letter to the Ephesians, encourages believers to put on the whole armour of God, and a very important part of that armour is 'the shield of faith' (Eph. 6:16). By faith, we are shielded from so many things by God's power 'until the coming of the salvation that is ready to be revealed in the last time' (1:5).

The nature of salvation
The word that is used for salvation in this verse (1:5) is the one that is used throughout the New Testament. However, the English Versions of the Bible do not bring out clearly the three-fold nature of salvation. If we are Christians, we have been saved, we are being saved and we will be saved. The day that we turned from our sin and put our faith in Jesus, we were saved. But salvation has a present continuous function; we go on being saved. This is what is known as sanctification, the process by which we become more like Jesus. Then there is the third aspect to salvation, the second coming of Jesus, when he will once again

break into human history. Then we will see the full fruit of that salvation.

The continuous dimension of salvation is important because if we miss it, we are left with what I call 'historic testimonies'. People say 'I came to Jesus when Billy Graham came to England in 1995'. Well, praise the Lord, but I want to know what he has done in their lives in the years that have followed. What is important is not just the moment when salvation becomes real but an ongoing walk with God.

The future is important because we have not yet received all the full blessings of the future age. Some of us were not healed when prayed for. We do not have completeness in every way. Many of us are blessed and touched by the power of the Spirit, but the day is coming when we will be absolutely perfect: body, mind and spirit. Every tear will be wiped away from our eyes. That day has not yet come, but we look to it with great anticipation.

A few years ago my grandmother had a party to celebrate her ninetieth birthday. About sixty people gathered and speeches were made about Grandma. One of the speakers turned to her and said, 'Well, Mrs. Gaukroger, here we are at your ninetieth birthday and we are looking forward to being here to celebrate your ninety-first.' Now Grandma had been unwell for many years and had staggered from one health crisis to another. So it was with a look of sheer disgust on her face that she replied, 'I do hope not!' There was a lengthy embarrassed pause after that retort, but all those close to her knew what she meant. On another occasion she said to me, 'Stephen, I wake up in the morning and am filled with an incredible sense of disappointment that I am still here. I want to go to a place where I am whole, where my mind is sharp, and where everything is right because I am with God.'

That is the salvation we are waiting for. We have not received it yet, but the thrilling thing about God's kingdom is that by faith we are seeing the blessings of the end time now through the power of his Spirit. We don't see it all, but we have a foretaste in the ongoing process of salvation.

Encouragement in our trials
Peter then continues his letter with some very simple points about our earthly struggles: 'In this [that is, in the three things we looked at that result from the new birth] you greatly rejoice, though now for a little while you may have to suffer grief in all kinds of trials' (1:6). The expression 'all kinds of trials' literally means multi-coloured. Peter describes our trials as coming in different shapes and sizes. However, later on in this letter Peter also talks of the multi-coloured grace of God (1 Pet. 4:10). How wonderful that in the multi-

coloured trials of life there is multi-coloured grace to cope with them. That is the thrilling truth that Peter never lets us get too far away from.

The reality of the struggle

Peter, however, is very realistic about the presence of trials. From time to time I meet Christians who have more in common with some aspects of Christian Science than with genuine Christianity in their wholesale denial of any kind of struggle in the Christian life. They imply that because Jesus has come into their lives, and they have been filled by the Holy Spirit, that all their problems are over. But when they do inevitably go through problems they develop a kind of schizophrenic dualism, a kind of denial of half of their life and the pain of what is going on. But Scripture is true to life. It doesn't require us to be involved in pretence. Trials will come. Jesus himself said, 'In this world you will have trouble. But take heart! I have overcome the world' (John 16:33). The Christian is not immune from the struggle. The first century believers were not and we will not be. Many struggle with the burden of failing health or unemployment or marital problems. Others with young families agonize over the thought of their children growing up in the kind of society we see around us today. And there are others who struggle with inner doubts and fears, and so on. But when we understand our living hope, our guaranteed inheritance and our certain protection, we can rise above those problems with the help of the family of God and the power of the Spirit in our lives.

The result of the struggle

Peter then goes on to describe the result of these trials. He writes: 'These have come so that your faith – of greater worth than gold, which perishes even though refined by fire – may be proved genuine and may result in praise, glory and honour when Jesus Christ is revealed' (1:7). When trials come, if we submit to God, the result will be that we will be refined in such a way that when Jesus come back, praise, honour and glory will be due to him because our lives will be a testimony to the strength which Jesus gives. Job's struggle is a good example of this. His circumstances were truly horrific yet his trust in God never wavered. One thing that really got to him, however, was that neither his wife nor his friends understood what he was going through. Sometimes we are able to cope with difficulties, but when people close to us don't understand, the effect can be devastating. However, if we keep holding on, by the power of God's Spirit, then one day our lives will be a testimony of the grace of God at work. One of the greatest witnesses to unbelievers is seeing the way Christians go through problems and how they cope by the grace of God. There is no need to pretend. You don't need to hold back the tears in case you let Jesus down. When people see us weeping they recognize our humanity, but they also see the grace of God in us where we can't see it in ourselves. And the result of the struggle is that in the future our lives will be a testimony of what Jesus did, even though we did not know it was happening. We do not need to put on a veneer of spirituality, we need to go through the struggle with the power of the Spirit, and then God works in us and the light shines in our lives.

The joy of the struggle
Peter then writes of a further encouragement we have as we face these many-coloured trials: 'Though you have not seen him, you love him; and even though you do not see him now, you believe in him [even in the midst of these struggles] and are filled with an inexpressible and glorious joy' (1:8). It's an inexpressible joy that comes when we have gone through the struggle and Jesus has been with us. It helps us to see Jesus. At the end of the book of Job, when he had come through all the struggles, he says, 'My ears had heard of you but now my eyes have seen you' (Job 42:5). His trials had transformed his faith from a second-hand belief, to an understanding and appreciation of the living God.

Knowing Jesus through the Word makes him more real than if he stood before us for all to see.

What an amazing concept. It destroys the logic of today's world, where 'seeing is believing'. In Christian things it is the other way round, believing is seeing. As we believe we get a new vision of this lovely Jesus. If I were to ask you who is more real, the person sitting next to you or Jesus, what would your answer be? The truth is, we are mere shadows compared to the reality of Jesus Christ. In heaven, through the weight of his glory, God will be very real.

There is a reality we cannot see. Greater than human physical existence, it is a reality of divine truth. Though we do not see him we love him, and when we really love him, we are filled with an inexpressible and glorious joy. Before my children had even been born I had learned to love them. Through each of the pregnancies I would see the babies grow, would feel them kick, and occasionally I would talk to them. And then when they were born, as each little child came into the world, I would see for the first time the person I already had begun to love. We have never seen Jesus, but one day, after years of gestation and struggle, we will see him as he bursts into view and we will know in that moment that we have loved him. And how much greater will the reality of that be than right now as we struggle to love him. We will see him as he is. Will not that be wonderful?

The reason for this inexpressible joy is that, as

Peter writes, 'you are receiving the goal of your faith, the salvation of your souls' (1:9). At the end of all our struggles, we will meet this glorious Jesus. Knowing him, loving him, every struggle will be at an end. There will be no more bitterness, no more pain, no more anguish, no more despair, no more disease. We will have reached our goal.

2

Salvation
(1 Peter 1:10-16)

In the previous chapter we looked at Peter's eagerness to encourage believers to develop an attitude of praise in the face of difficult circumstances, and to see trials and hardship as part of a refining process that will result in 'praise, glory and honour' when Jesus returns.

In the first three verses of the section which is the subject of this chapter, Peter's burden is to persuade believers that the hope of salvation is not a vain hope. He writes:

> Concerning this salvation, the prophets, who spoke of the grace that was to come to you, searched intently and with greatest care, trying to find out the time and circumstances to which the Spirit of Christ in them was pointing when he predicted the sufferings of Christ and the glories that would follow. It was revealed to them that they were not serving themselves but you, when they spoke of the things that have now been told you by those who have preached the gospel to you by the Holy Spirit sent from heaven. Even angels long to look into these things (1 Pet. 1:10-12).

Salvation in prophecy and preaching

Our salvation has been both prophesied and preached. Peter writes that the prophets 'searched intently and with the greatest care'. Reading that phrase I am reminded of the Bereans in the Acts of the Apostles. These people didn't only listen to the apostle Paul's teaching, but searched the Scriptures daily to see if what he said was true. The prophets had impressions from God, direct words whispered in their ears, but they were not some kind of human dictating machines for God. He used their personality, he used their character to grapple with the things of Jehovah, the great God of the Bible. So they searched hard to know, and in their searching, God revealed himself to them.

And so we get wonderful prophesies in the Old Testament of the time when this salvation is to come. In Isaiah 53 we find a wonderful example of this. Isaiah talks of the suffering servant, of someone who would come who would be broken, and the result of his brokenness will be salvation. Isaiah could not have understood the full depth of what he wrote; he just had a vague glimmer of what was to come.

Another example of this type of prophecy is found in Micah 5:2: Hundreds of years before the event, Micah prophesied that a ruler for Israel would be born in Bethlehem. There is a pun there that is lost on us today. Bethlehem means 'house of bread' and it would be in this very place that the Bread of Life, Jesus, would be born. Hundreds of years before this happened the prophet Micah foretells that truth.

So our salvation is not an invention or creation of the first century, it was prophesied by God years before. Our God had salvation in mind from before the dawn of time, it was not some last minute rescue plan. It had always been in his heart to deal with the initial rebellion into which Adam and Eve led the whole human race.

Not only was this salvation prophesied, however, verse 12 tells us that it was preached. 'It was revealed to them that they were not serving themselves but you, when they spoke of the things that have now been told you by those who have preached the gospel to you by the Holy Spirit sent from heaven' (1:12). This is not good news of man's invention – it was placed into the hearts of the prophets by the living God and it was also placed into the minds of the recipients of the first century by anointed preachers of the Word.

There never will be a time, until the second coming, when preachers are redundant. The message is to be preached, to be explained. When the Word of God is preached it is part of a great line of history reaching back to the prophets and preachers of old who explained the good news of the kingdom of God.

Then, at the end of verse 12, Peter adds: 'Even

angels long to look into these things'. A more literal translation of the Greek might be 'even angels long to stoop down to get a better view'. The angels long to get down to our level, as it were, to understand these things for themselves. Unlike humans, they are not recipients of God's saving grace. But they long to be more than spirit attendants to the King of Kings; they want to understand and rejoice in the great message of salvation.

If we want to live successfully in a dangerous world, we are going to have to live differently from the world. Success in the world's eyes is seen as achieving status and power. But Jesus demonstrated that the way to succeed is not by being thought of as great, but by humbling oneself (Phil. 2:6-11). If we want to be successful we need to turn upside-down all the things which the world believes makes a person successful. There are five things in particular that I want us to look at: we are under starter's orders, we are under control, our faith is under guarantee, we are acting under authority, and our lives are under review.

Under starter's orders
Peter writes: 'Prepare your minds for action' (1:13). We are under starter's orders. We do not know what the future will bring, we do not know where it will take us, but we know that we are in

God's hands. The King James Version translates this phrase as 'Gird up the loins of your mind.' This rather archaic rendering translates the original very helpfully because in the ancient world to gird up your loins meant to tuck one's robes up into one's belt, and this was the usual way of making the standard garment more practical for working in, or running in. If you neglected to do so, it would trip you up or hamper your ability to work effectively. The modern equivalent perhaps is the expression 'to roll your sleeves up'.

Many believers have forgotten that they are under starter's orders. They are taking their time in the changing room; they are wandering around the track, chatting to the spectators; they are musing with officials about the state of the weather, and if the race will be run or not. But they are not ready for action. So Peter charges us to get ready. This is not the time to be lounging around, this is the time to live. Holy living demands that believers move away from being spectators to being participants in the Christian life. Any church will be successful only as far as every believer is both a worshipper and a worker. There is no room for passengers on the gospel train. We are to be girding our minds, preparing ourselves for action. We are not to be those who go to church Sunday by Sunday simply to worship and hear the word expounded. The goal of our lives should be to go into the world, filled by the Spirit, empowered by the Word, to serve him and be salt and light wherever we find ourselves. That is our goal, so be ready for action.

Under control
The next phrase in verse 13 is 'be self-controlled'. The older translations say 'be sober' and the original word was used almost exclusively in the ancient world to mean avoidance of alcoholic indulgence. But as time went on, and particularly in the New Testament, the word came to mean to be self-controlled in general. So Peter says if you want to make an impact in your world, not only have you to be ready for action, but secondly, you have to be self-controlled. Christians have the Holy Spirit's power to help them be self-controlled. The Bible nowhere forbids the drinking of alcohol, but it is quite clear that being out of control in relation to alcohol is wrong and that drunkenness is not an appropriate form of behaviour for the believer. Instead, we are to be filled with the Holy Spirit and have his control in our lives.

Many believers, however, have something else controlling their lives. We are dominated by fears, by dependencies of various kinds, by lusts and cravings, and so on. And that is why, to live successfully in this dangerous world, in order to model freedom to those around us who are imprisoned by sin, we ourselves must be free in order to be self-controlled.

Under guarantee
The third point I want to draw out is that our salvation is underwritten, under guarantee. Peter writes: 'Set your hope fully on the grace to be given you when Jesus Christ is revealed' (1:13b). Christians all over the world who are persecuted for their faith, and who are struggling to live successfully for Christ in this dangerous world, should focus, not on the immediate, not even exclusively on their relationship with Jesus, but on the hope that when the end of the world comes they will be in his hands. Then every wrong will be righted, every bad thing will be sorted out. Place your hope in that guarantee. Our hope is not in an opinion or a philosophy, it is in the certainty that human history is *his story*. And it is a story that is going to be played out on the stage of earth for just as long as God intends, and not for a minute longer.

Hope is the one thing that keeps us going perhaps more than anything else. Why? Because we can stand almost anything if we know that it is going to finish. The problem with many illnesses is that the pain goes on and on without any let up. Even a small pain can be very debilitating if it goes on and on. But our hope is that, no matter what happens now, there is an underwritten, guaranteed, fail-safe destiny. If we understand this, it will grip us in the depths of our soul. All the troubles, all the hassles of life, are put in the right perspective, because Jesus is coming.

Under authority

Peter points out in verse 14 that we are under authority: 'As obedient children ...' Believers are children who do as they are told. In the first century, the obedience of children was taken for granted. Two thousand years later, our culture has moved far away from that view. Most Christian parents no doubt long for the help of God in their home. 'Which of us is wise enough for this task?' we ask ourselves. Yet the Bible calls us to be obedient children, doing what our heavenly Father says. The way some Christians treat his commands can only be described as the pick and mix approach. If they think a verse fits, they apply it and if it doesn't, they don't. But God calls us to sit under the authority of the Word as obedient children and to do what he says. We may not always understand why, but we trust God, because we know he sees the big picture.

The sentence which began 'As obedient children' continues 'do not conform to the evil desires you had when you lived in ignorance'. The question here is who or what determines the way we behave? In the ancient world, as today, people were held captive by their desires. In many ways it was a horrific time in which to live. We think the world today is worse than it has ever been. But that is not true. Standards certainly have been declining during this century, but in the ancient world there were moral and ethical atrocities on an unbelievable scale. Waste and gluttony were rife. One ancient historian, describing a first century feast, tells how two thousand fish and seven thousand birds were consumed by a crowd of about a hundred people. The Romans would eat for days at a time and make themselves sick between courses in order to gorge more food. This was no polite or gentle society, but one that was dominated by their appetites. It was a corrupt world, a world driven by sexual excess, a world where homosexuality and lesbianism was rife; a world where sexual experimentation with both animals and children was common in aristocratic circles. This was not a world of polite gentility, or a world where everything was in order. But it was the world in which ordinary believers had to live and Peter charges them not to be controlled by their lusts, desires and appetites.

We cannot afford to be judgmental about Christians who fall, because we know the pressures we are all under. Instead we reach out with love and tenderness because we are sorry they have fallen, and because we know that it is only by God's grace that we have been kept from falling. Peter's words are not a call to judgmentalism, but a challenge to us as obedient children to bring our lives into line with God's Word.

Under review

Fifthly, Peter says, 'But just as he who called you is holy, so be holy in all you do; for it is written: "Be holy, because I am holy"' (1:15-16). The quotation in verse 16 is from Leviticus (11:44, 45; 19:2; 20:7) where we find the call to Israel to be holy because their God is holy. Our lives are constantly being brought under review in comparison with God. How easy it is to justify almost everything we do by comparison with somebody else. We say, 'Well I might be bad, Lord, but I am not half as bad as so-and-so.' So we make a point of comparison with other people. But God, with his immense understanding of the human condition, robs us all of that excuse and says, 'No, it's not the apostles or other Christians you should be comparing yourself with, it is with me. Be holy, for I am holy.'

Holiness, however, cannot be defined as a series of negatives: Christians don't go to places like that; Christians don't do things like that, and so on. Holiness is being like Jesus. Jesus constantly went to what the religious people of his day considered the 'wrong' places, he did the 'wrong' things and said the 'wrong' things to the 'wrong' people. In Luke 7:36-50, when Jesus was dining at the house of Simon the Pharisee, a woman 'who had led a sinful life in that town', presumably as a prostitute, anointed his feet. The Pharisee was shocked and said to himself, 'If this man were a prophet, he would know she is a sinner' (7:39). But Jesus knew, and forgave her lovingly. Why was it that the despised and hated members of society flocked to Jesus, while the religious leaders hated him? The religious leaders had made up certain rules of holiness which declared certain places and people as out of bounds. Evangelicals over recent years have been very muddled about this too, and have retreated from the arts, from economics, from politics, and from a whole range of things which they deemed as no-go areas. But when we went out, the world rushed in. We created a kind of spiritual power vacuum, and now the job of the church is to get back in and to get its hands dirty, not compromising our essential committedness to the living God, but being in there with the difficult tasks of our world today. Being holy in the hard places, being holy not by virtue of the way we dress or our language or vocabulary, but being holy because he who has called us is holy.

In Leviticus, holiness was seen as separation from sin, and our holiness is also seen as separation from sin, not physical separation particularly, but an empowerment that shows our lives radiant with God's presence. Holiness, properly understood, is an immensely attractive thing to Christians and non-Christians because there is a warmth about it, an awareness but not a tolerance of sin. Jesus demonstrated this when the religious leaders brought before him a woman taken in adultery. He didn't deny her sin, but said to her accusers, 'If any one of you is without sin, let him be the first to throw the first stone' (John 8:7).

So our lives are constantly under review. Week by week we attend church, day by day we read the Bible and pray and think thoughts about our Lord. But we need to do more than simply go through the motions. We need to bring our lives back to God and place them on the altar and say, 'God, here I am. I am happy to be open to the searchlight of your gaze into my life. Come and reveal in me any wicked way. Search me and know me and lead me in the way of everlasting. Help me to know that I am walking in holiness.'

What a privilege to live that kind of successful life in a dangerous world. It may not sound like success in worldly terms, but it is the only kind of success that matters. It is the success that sees us ready for action, under control, under the guarantee that nothing will rob us of the salvation we have, under the authority of God to live out his desires, and under constant review to live holy lives. What a thrill it is to be part of the kingdom where the Spirit longs to give us those assurances.

3

A Secure Life
(1 Peter 1:17–2:3)

The writings of the Apostle Paul are those of a systematic theologian, with each phrase following the previous one with unquestionable logic. This letter written by the Apostle Peter, however, is more in the nature of a rambling sermon. There is a degree of repetition and changing patterns of thought that put us in mind of a pastor engaging with the needs of his flock, encouraging them so that they may be able to live successfully in this dangerous world. So as we look at this passage we will not go through it in verse order but will follow the different themes that Peter dwells on.

Believers are secure
Peter is at pains to help the believers to understand that their salvation is secure even though their faith appears to be based on something new. In some respects the ancient world was not so different from ours. Faced with something new, there were two responses commonly made, then as now: 'If it's new it must be wrong!' and 'If it's new it won't last!' Christianity fell into this category.

For many of the ancient world, Christianity seemed like a last minute thought or idea. But Peter tells his readers that this is not so. He writes in verse 20: 'He was chosen before the creation of the world, but was revealed in these last times for your sake.' God's plan to save the world in Jesus Christ is not something new, it predates all other religious viewpoints. Nothing predates the mind of God and so our faith is secure because it has this eternal origin. Jesus and the salvation he would bring were in the mind of God long before the dawn of time itself. What an immensely reassuring thought.

The second typical response of 'If it's new it won't last' is also dealt with by Peter. God's salvation has a certain future. In verse 18 Peter says: 'For you know it was not with perishable things such as silver or gold that you were redeemed ...'. The irony in Peter's words may be lost on us, but it would have been significant to these early believers. Silver and gold were items that were thought of as lasting and not perishable. Peter's point is that we have been redeemed by what is more permanent than silver or gold.

Then in verse 23 Peter writes: 'For you have been born again, not of perishable seed.' The word *seed* and the word *semen* have the same root, and Peter points out that death is present even in conception. That might sound quite morbid to you, but it is a reminder that we all have within us the seeds of perishability. The believer, however, has been born again, not of perishable seed, but of imperishable.

Peter's imagery changes again in verses 24 and 25. Don't just look at silver or gold, don't just look at the human being, but look at nature itself:

> All men are like grass,
> and all their glory is like the flowers of the field;
> the grass wither and the flowers fall,
> but the word of the Lord stands for ever.

This teaching revealed by God will last. Gold and silver will be corrupted, human beings will eventually die, grass will wither and flowers will fade, but the word of the Lord endures for ever. Our salvation is secure for it is founded on something that will never, never fail.

In addition to security there are four practical things that our salvation should result in.

Reverent fear

'Since you call on a Father who judges each man's work impartially, live your lives as strangers here in reverent fear' (1:17). Our response to the God who thought about us in eternity past and who will not forget about is in eternity future should be one of reverent fear. We are in grave danger of becoming too pally with the Almighty and we have, to use James Packer's words, built ourselves a pygmy God and therefore we have become pygmy Christians. In all the ordinariness of our everyday lives God wants us to come and see him in all of his splendour. True, he is our Father, but he is also our judge and we are to deal with him in reverent fear. The key to holiness in the twentieth-century church is a new fear of God, not a craven, bullied fear, but one which flows out of reverence.

Fervent love

> 'Now that you have purified yourselves by obeying the truth so that you have sincere love for your brothers, love one another deeply, from the heart' (1:22).

Because the Holy Spirit has shed abroad God's love in our hearts, we are to love one another. It's very important to understand that this passage does not call upon us to *like* one another, but to *love* one another. There may be times when we find fellow Christians irritating and annoying. Is that an excuse to stop loving them? No! It should be the trigger to loving them more. The harder people are to get on with, the more they need loving. That is the revolutionary nature of Christian love.

The New Testament draws on a variety of words to speak of love: erotic love, brotherly love, family love and so on. But when it comes to the love which originates in the heart of God, the New Testament stressed a special word, *agape*. Agape is a love which is not motivated by selfish ends, and this is very important. This love of which Peter speaks is entirely altruistic, it is a love which loves for Christ's sake and is sincere. Christians need to be a people that so love one another, not in a soppy or sentimental way, but in a deep way that involves commitment to one another, that people will be drawn to us. That kind of love is infectious, for people long to be part of a family where they are loved.

Still to do with relationships, however, we are then given a list here of five things we are to rid ourselves of. This brings us to the third practical result of our salvation: right relationships.

Right relationships
True salvation should result in right relationships, so we are to rid ourselves of malice, deceit, hypocrisy, envy and slander (2:1). We should have no problem understanding what all these words mean, the problem is allowing the Spirit to give us the power to rid ourselves of these things. These sins are all relational sins, they are sins within the body of Christ, they are the damage we do to each other; they are not private sins we engage in that have no impact on the rest of the body of Christ. Peter says the trouble is, if we don't live in reverent fear and don't love one another, there will be this negative explosion of malice, deceit and so on, because the self-life, the carnal life will remain

alive within us. It needs to be put to death in order that these things are not present among us.

The subtlety of these things is evident in every fellowship. Take envy, for example. It can be overcome by a Christian in the obvious areas and yet succumbed to in the not so obvious areas. We may ask God to help us not to be jealous of others' possessions and may experience real freedom from covetousness on that level. But often there is a more subtle temptation, the temptation to wonder why we have not been given a position of leadership or authority, or been chosen for a particular task, or given a certain responsibility when we feel that we have been called. Such things breed hurt in a church, they breed pain. Envy of those who seem to have arrived is very strong in the church today.

How we need right relationships in our churches! We need to deal with these things in a sensitive and godly way. We must repent before God of our part in bad relationships and seek to move on in him. Rid yourselves of all malice and all deceit, hypocrisy, envy and slander.

A craving for God

The fourth thing that our salvation should result in is found in 2:2: 'Like newborn babies, crave pure spiritual milk, so that by it you may grow in your salvation.' This is a lovely, homely metaphor. A newborn baby is desperate for milk, it craves for it. And that is how we should be towards the things of God. One of the characteristics of godliness that Peter draws us to, if we are to live successfully in this dangerous world, is a craving for God. The desperation we feel should be like that described in that lovely incident in the Old Testament where Jacob wrestled with the Angel and he says, 'I will not let you go unless you bless me' (Gen. 32:26). That is the passion God wants to breed in the church of Jesus, 'I won't let you go, Lord, until you bless me.'

We crave, we long, like a new born for milk, to know God's love and power in our lives. We must not be prepared any longer to settle for mediocrity or the average or the ordinary, we must not be prepared to settle for the second best. We must crave for pure spiritual nourishment in our lives, and when we do we will discover that 'the Lord is good' (2:2).

So we are secure because God's eternal love for us and commitment to us will never end. But he longs for us to have a reverent fear for him; he longs for us to have a sincere love for one another; he longs for us to be in right relationships with one another; and he longs for us to be thirsty for him. When we have these attitudes to God and one another, we will be able to live successfully in a dangerous world.

4

Jesus, the Rock
(1 Peter 2:4-8)

Peter's readers in a difficult world; they were very much a minority; and emperor worship was mandatory for Roman citizens. Many Christians died because they were unwilling to make that kind of allegiance to any other than the God who was revealed in Jesus Christ. It seems odd to us now but the first-century Christians were thought of largely as atheistic. This was because their God could not be seen, and therefore it was deemed he did not exist. Ancient gods were very much seen. So Christians were an alienated minority, struggling to make their mark in a world which viewed any kind of aberration from the norm as very threatening indeed. Certainly the world did not have the *laisser-faire* approach that we see today, the attitude that says, 'Believe what you want, it is up to you.' A person who held to a different belief system was considered a disloyal citizen, at least potentially. The first century believers were marginalised in their society, barred from the decision-making structures of the day, kept on the edge of the chambers of commerce and the local political systems. These believers, struggling in the dangerous and difficult world, needed encouragement. And that is just what Peter gave them in the passionate and pastoral way of his, talking about their Jesus who understood what it was to be marginalised, alienated and rejected. Therefore they would face the difficult times with confidence because their Leader, their Saviour, the one from whom they had taken their name, also experienced pain and rejection. But more than that, he had the power to something about it in their lives. And so this passage is one of the most Christocentric passages of all. It is all about Jesus.

As you come to him, the living Stone – rejected by men but chosen by God and precious to him – you also, like living stones, are being built into a spiritual house to be a holy priesthood, offering spiritual sacrifices acceptable to God through Jesus Christ. For in Scripture it says:
> 'See, I lay a stone in Zion,
>> a chosen and precious cornerstone,
> and the one who trusts in him
>> will never be put to shame.'

Now to you who believe, this stone is precious. But to those who do not believe,
> 'The stone the builders rejected
>> has become the capstone,'

and,
> 'A stone that causes men to stumble,
>> and a rock that makes them fall.'

They stumble because they disobey the message – which is also what they were destined for.

The Living Stone

This expression that Peter uses in verse 4 seems to contain a contradiction: stones don't live. So why did Peter choose to express himself in this way? Peter is reminding his readers that Jesus, the foundation for their lives as believers, is not an abstract, philosophical theory, but is real, rock-like, and utterly dependable. The foundation stone of our faith is not an 'it' but a 'he'. He is *living*. Jesus has all the living-ness, the aliveness of God in his person and all the stability and reliability of a huge rock which cannot be lifted. He is not a mere stone who does not understand us. He is not an impersonal, unfeeling Saviour, but a Saviour who relates to us right where we are. There is no need for pretence, for God knows us completely.

Yet he was rejected by men, people didn't want him. 'He came to that which was his own, but his own did not receive him' (John 1:11). Jesus was rejected by his own and yet he is precious to God, Peter tells us.

Stones with the Spirit

Peter also tells us, in verse 5, that because we believe in Jesus we too become stones with the same Spirit. And we are being built into 'a *spiritual* house', not a physical house, 'to be a holy priesthood, offering spiritual sacrifices acceptable to God through Jesus Christ'.

Peter, writing this, may have had in mind that

his name, which means 'Rock', had been given to him by Jesus. But he is telling his readers that they are all rocks or stones, they all have this stability because Jesus came into their lives. Today, Christians can become imbalanced when they emphasize either stability or spirituality to the exclusion of the other. But, we are to be both living and rocks. God is calling us to a rock-like stability as Jesus dominates our lives, and also to a suppleness, a sensitivity, a responsiveness to his Holy Spirit.

So, as living stones, we are being built into a spiritual house. We need each other; a brick on its own is useless. There is no solitariness about the church of Jesus. We need each other: the spiritually mature, the spiritually immature; the old, the young; the struggling, the not struggling; the intelligent, the less intelligent; the academically gifted, the less gifted. All are necessary in this spiritual building. There is a place for each of us – stones with the Spirit.

A precious Corner stone

In verse 6 we come across the term 'corner stone' and in verse 7 the word 'capstone', which can also mean 'corner stone'. There seem to be two possible meanings for this word. It could mean either the foundation stone, a very sizeable stone on which a building rested, or else it could mean the final stone that is positioned at the very top of a building, rather like the battlements of a castle. From the scant evidence we have from the ancient world, certain analysis is impossible. But, whether it is the foundation or some other kind of special stone, what is clear is the picture of the builders in a quarry, assessing the various stones and picking some but rejecting a particular stone, the stone that is ultimately going to be the crown and glory of the building.

Peter is reminding believers that when they suffer rejection they should remember Jesus. He was rejected, but he has become the corner stone. He was rejected, but he ended up being the most significant of all – there is no greater than he. Remember that, when you are feeling down and discouraged, for 'the one who trusts in him will never be put to shame' (2:6). When we put our trust in the cornerstone, it does not mean we will no longer make mistakes. We will fail, we will have problems. But those who put their trust in Jesus will never be put to shame. Their eternal destiny will not be in doubt, he will never let them down. I urge you to bring your needs to this rock who will never fail you and on whom you can place your certainty and security. What a Saviour we have.

Children have an innate trust of their parents. My children like to play a game where they stand on the stairs and jump into my arms. Sometimes they will go up two steps or three. But on one occasion, one of them went up to the sixth step. When I told him it wasn't a good idea, he said, 'Why not, Daddy? I trust you. You will catch me.' But there comes a point when trust in a human father would not be sustainable. Despite how my child felt, I was not capable to meet his level of trust. The thing that thrills me, however, about our heavenly Father is that no matter how much our level of trust rises, he will meet that trust. He can't be defeated, he can't be put to shame by our requests.

In verse 7 we read, 'Now to you who believe, this stone is precious. But to those who do not believe, [he has become] a rock that makes them fall.' Peter continues with his building metaphor. An expert can look at a stone and see its value and significance. An amateur can look at the same stone and see just a rock. Perspective is very important. If you believe, then Jesus is precious; if you don't believe, he is not. That is why some people can take the name of Jesus in vain, can dismiss him, can be incredibly negative about the gospel. They do not understand why we love Jesus and how much he means to us. To those who believe, he is increasingly precious.

The Stone the builders rejected
Jesus turned all the values of the ancient world on their head. Most of the people didn't think he was important, but in actual fact, he is the most

significant person ever to have lived. Christians may be in the minority at any given period of history, but one day every knee will bow and every tongue confess that Jesus Christ is Lord (Phil. 2:10, 11). Every person who has blasphemed the name of Jesus, everyone who has rejected the Son of God and whose value system is wholly opposed to Scripture, everyone who has ever ridiculed believers for their faith, all will kneel one day before Jesus. The day is coming when the whole universe will see what has always been true, that though Jesus was rejected by men, he was approved by God and is precious to him.

Our world is a world of topsy-turvy values. Many live their entire lives with the wrong expectations and values. Family life is not valued highly. Honesty and integrity are not valued highly. We are turned upside down. What Jesus wants to do, however, is to come into our world and turn everything the right way up. He wants to be the radical re-orderer of priorities, for although he is the stone that has been rejected, he is, in fact, the corner stone, the most important stone.

The Stone we cannot ignore
In verse 8 Peter quotes from Isaiah 8:14:

> 'A stone that causes men to stumble
> and a rock that makes them fall.'

Jesus cannot be ignored: when you encounter

54

Jesus, something happens; either he crushes all that is self in you and replaces it with his Spirit, or you fall over the stone. Jesus is the touchstone of all that is reality, and so he has become a rock of offence for many people. Jesus causes people to stumble because he is so plain about his claims. The statements he makes are consistently in exclusive terms. For example, he says, 'I am the way and the truth and the life. No-one comes to the Father except through me' (John 14:6). Now you can't help but stumble over that verse. Jesus is either the only way to God, or else what he claims is nonsense. There is no middle ground.

We live in a pluralistic world where any number of religious viewpoints vie for our attention. Jesus is offensive because he claims to be exclusively the way to God. And so we find ourselves out of kilter with the feeling of modern culture which is geared to tolerance with regard to the claims of different religious leaders. My prayer is that the Jesus who is the cornerstone of history, the apex of all that really matters, will increasingly exert his influence in our culture and society and will increasingly be acknowledged. Don't you long for this?

To those who do believe, he is precious. But everyone who disobeys this message is bound to stumble, their lives won't work, they won't get it together properly. Why? Because the very thing they need to complete the building of their life, they have already rejected. It is our job to point them back to Jesus, the one who makes sense of it all. And what a thrill it is when people meet Jesus, for they stop stumbling over him and instead they find him to be a rock on which they can build their lives.

5

Christians Together

(1 Peter 2:9-10)

Sometimes, modern English translations of the Bible are limited in conveying precisely what the original languages mean. In old English, for example, it was possible to distinguish between 'you' singular and 'you' plural, whereas in modern English 'you' is used for both singular and plural. In 2:9 'you' is plural:

> 'But you are a chosen people, a royal priesthood, a holy nation, a people belonging to God, that you may declare the praises of him who called you out of darkness into his wonderful light' (2:9).

This is a reminder that most of the New Testament letters are addressed to groups of people rather than isolated individuals. The New Testament is written generally in the context of body life. We do not live out our Christian lives in isolation. The New Testament knows nothing of solitary Christianity, instead it sees us constantly in a framework of the body of Christ. For all our differences we are together as the family of God. Peter in this verse describes four things that Christians are together.

A chosen people

Do you ever look at members of your own family and wonder how you could all be so different? I am reminded of the saying 'You can choose your friends, but you can't choose your family.' It is the same in God's family. We didn't choose one another, but God did. We are a chosen people.

The older translations refer to this phrase as 'an elect' nation. The Jews knew about election, but wrongly believed themselves to be better than other people because they had been chosen by God. They were very dismissive of the Gentile nations, calling them Barbarians. There was an arrogance about their attitude. Peter was at pains, however, to point out that the Asian Christians that being chosen by God should not lead to arrogance, but to humility.

Every person in twentieth-century Britain needs love, acceptance, security and purpose. Peter makes this possible by showing what the church of Jesus is. We are a chosen people.

I can remember occasions at school as a child when sports teams were being chosen. The teacher would assign two captains to pick the teams. The sporting ones had no worries about being chosen, but emotions would start to rise and panic would set in as the number left got smaller and smaller. If you are not a sporting person you may well remember the embarrassment of knowing you were going to be the last one to be picked. Yet you were desperate to be chosen.

As Christians we are a chosen people. Even if the world rejects our values, even if we as individuals feel rejected in our place of work, or in our family, we need to remind ourselves we have been chosen by God. He loves us and longs for us to know that we are special to him in his family.

A royal priesthood

Secondly, Peter says, we are 'a royal priesthood'. This would have been a terribly shocking thing to the first century people. Peter was saying as Christians we are all priests together, we all have a role, be we men or woman, old or young, Jew or Gentile. Whoever comes to know Jesus becomes a kingly priest serving in God's court. Each has a role to play; each one has a value.

Many Christians struggle with a sense of uselessness, they feel they have nothing to grab hold of, no certainty of what they are about. But God says they have a value, a special role. Each as a priest can intercede for others and be involved in this special ministry. You may not have been chosen by any individual, be it a partner, a parent or a friend. God himself has chosen you for a particular aspect of royal service.

Whoever you are, whatever your background, whatever damage there may have been done in your life up to this point, however other people may view you and your gifts, God has a role for you in his royal priesthood – a serving role. Every believer is called to be a priest, a worker in the kingdom of God. That is what is so exciting about being part of God's family. We've not just been chosen, but we have also been given a commissioning, a function.

We are all valued in this family. It is so hard to believe that in the church sometimes, because we feel insignificant and pushed aside, we feel that we do not have anything significant to contribute, and that is debilitating. But God has given us a role, he has selected us to serve him.

A holy nation

Thirdly, we are 'a holy nation'. The word 'holy' means 'set apart'; we are a distinctive people. It does not mean we are becoming that, rather we are holy *already*. So we have to live out the truth of that statement.

Holiness doesn't depend on our ability to be good, it is dependent on God's ability to fill us with his Holy Spirit. There is no limiting his power. We see it at work in Mark Magdalene, a person horribly compromised with demonic activity, a woman of very low repute in every way. But Jesus touched her life. You can imagine her wondering at this: 'Me, a holy person, after all I have done? Are you serious?' Yet it is with people like her and people like us that Jesus is building his church into a holy nation. No-one is too bad, too dirty, too low to play a part, for holiness is not of us, but of God.

Christians today have the task of presenting a model of holiness to a world where sexual promiscuity, financial permissiveness, business irregularity, and a lack of integrity pervades every level of society. What society needs is not simply the condemning words of a church which demands repentance, though it needs that, but it also needs a model of a different way of community living. We are the alternative society, we are those who will provide a genuine sense of being a community together, a holy nation. I have always been impressed by the words engraved on the Statue of Liberty in New York: 'Give me your tired, your poor, your huddled masses yearning to breathe free, the wretched refuse of your teeming shore. Send these, the homeless, tempest tossed to me. I lift my lamp beside the golden door.' And if that can be said of a nation, surely it can be said of the church. 'Bring me the wretched, the desperate, the struggling,' says Jesus, 'and I will make them into a holy nation.'

The church is not for the strong, it is for the weak. In God's sight we are all weak but he wants to build us up into a pure and holy nation.

A people belonging to God

The Jews were constantly trying to identify historical connections, for ancestry meant a great deal and it was an issue of honour for them. Knowing their ancestry, where one fitted in, was very affirming. There is a great need in every human soul to belong somewhere. But for many people in our society this affirmation is lacking. Society has become so dislocated that people often don't feel they have any roots. They don't know where they belong or where they fit in.

The people to whom Peter wrote were in a similar state. They were a displaced people, far from home, in a strange land. But Peter encourages them that they do belong, they are a people who belong to God. They belong to an invisible reality, to a nation they cannot see, to a kingdom they cannot touch with their hands, but one that is more real than the kingdom they are living in right now. They belong to God.

Christians today often feel a sense of unbelonging in our world, for we are strangers and pilgrims here. But we are members of another kingdom, a kingdom where we will feel utterly at home, where there will be no conflict concerning what we believe. We belong to God.

This is what it means to be a member of the kingdom of the living God. We are a chosen people, a royal priesthood, a holy nation, a people belonging to God.

Declaring God's praise

After these four descriptions of who we are as believers, Peter then gives us the reason why God has made us so: 'that you may declare the praises of him who called you out of darkness into his wonderful light' (2:9). The whole purpose of these privileges is to encourage us to praise God, to thank him that he has chosen us, that we belong to him, that we have a role to play in his royal priesthood, that we can be part of his holy nation. Our hearts should ring out in praise to God.

These truths do something deep in our being and lead us into praise of God. People's outward response will be different, according to their different personalities. Some will be very expressive and demonstrative, others quieter and more reserved – but there must be praise, there must be gratitude to God for all he has done. A grateful believer is an honour to God, and an ungrateful believer is a travesty of what the Christian faith is about.

What has God done? He has delivered us out of darkness into his wonderful light. Once we were blind, but now we can see. It's as if a light has been turned on in a dark room, flooding it with God's glorious light. And the world of the first century was very dark indeed, full of horror and fear. But into that dark world, God shone his light in the person of his Son. For some, becoming a Christian is a very dramatic, Damascus Road kind of experience. For others, it is a much more gradual process. Whatever our experience, light has dawned and the darkness has been dispelled.

Peter writes: 'Once you were not a people, but now you are the people of God; once you had not received mercy, but now you have received mercy' (2:10). This verse is a reference back to the book of Hosea. The message of Hosea is about rescue.

God told Hosea to go and rescue Gomer from prostitution. He marries her and they have two children, one called 'Not a People' and the other called 'Not Receiving Mercy'. These, of course, are the meanings of their names, and in the Bible, names meant a great deal. Hosea named his children in this way as a prophetic sign to Israel. Yet he rescues his wife and brings her back into the family home once more when she returns to prostitution. In so doing he behaves in a way that contradicts his children's names and gives us a picture of how God feels about us. He is a God of mercy – they were not a people, now they are a people.

The gospel is a great leveller. It tells us that all of us were once dead in our sins, which means that none of us are better than any other at the foot of the Cross. Dead people cannot do anything to help themselves. But Jesus gives us new life, and as a people we have that life living within us. We have received the overflowing mercy of God.

Because we have received mercy, it is possible for us together to be his chosen people, a royal priesthood, all of us having a role of serving and caring for one another. Because of his mercy we can be a holy nation, a community with standards that are different from the rest of society, with values that are based on God's Word. Because of his mercy we know that we belong to him.

So we go into a dangerous world full of assurance, confident that God will help us be what he has called us to be.

6

Living in Two Worlds
(1 Peter 2:11-17)

As we saw in the previous chapter, Peter stressed
to these scattered believers that they were a chosen
people, a holy nation, a people belonging to and
special to God. Now he continues:

> 'Dear friends, I urge you, as aliens and strangers
> in the world, to abstain from sinful desires, which
> war against your soul. Live such good lives among
> the pagans that, though they accuse you of doing
> wrong, they may see your good deeds and glorify
> God on the day he visits us' (1:11-12).

The believer's dual citizenship
At the outset of this passage we find another
example of the warmth of feeling Peter has
towards these believers in Asia. 'Dear friends' he
calls them. They are not mere colleagues or
acquaintances, they are his friends.

In his next words, however, he refers to them
as 'aliens and strangers' in the world. This tension
between belonging to God and being a stranger
in the world is something we have already come
across in the very first verse of this letter. Peter is

constantly trying to balance this tension of being friends of God on the one hand and strangers in the world on the other. Theirs was a dangerous world. The Nero persecutions, which began shortly after this letter was sent, probably resulted in the deaths of both Paul and Peter. The church went from having a relatively privileged position to being a persecuted minority. So for the recipients of this letter it was a dangerous world in which to live, and history has shown that it became increasingly difficult for believers in the decades towards the end of the first century. So Peter urges them never to forget that in this dangerous world, their ultimate citizenship is not of the earth but it is with God in heaven. The actual words used are 'temporary residents' – those who are just passing through.

Most people know what it feels like to be living in a place temporarily, from holidays or visits or whatever. In such a situation we relate differently to our surroundings than we would if we were there permanently. We find it easier to put up with inconveniences and discomforts because we know we will have to endure them only for a short while. That's how it is for Christians in this world: we are temporary residents; things will feel uncomfortable for a while and we won't feel entirely at home, because our home is somewhere else. We are not citizens primarily of earth, we are citizens of a far more wonderful place, and a far greater destiny awaits us. So in our relationship with the state we must not forget we have a higher loyalty.

The first century political authorities recognized this very clearly and that is why they found the church such a threat. Believers were seen as insurrectionists, rebels, traitors and generally were considered to be untrustworthy and unreliable. The Christians would not say 'Caesar is Lord', they would only say that Jesus is Lord. They would not make this oath to Caesar because only Jesus had the ultimate claim on their lives. Today, believers in many countries in the world are persecuted because the authorities recognize that Christians answer to a higher authority than the state.

We are, however, citizens of the country in which we live as well as being citizens of a higher kingdom. And if we are to live right in the earthly kingdom, we must have personal integrity. So Peter writes: 'Abstain from sinful desires, which war against your soul' (2:11). We are to be model citizens in this regard, and not let the sin which pervades society as a whole infiltrate our lives. We are to be set apart, so when people look at us they see a quality of life which cannot be aped or mimicked anywhere else. Personal integrity comes as we recognize we are friends of God, that his Spirit lives within us and we are different people. We have a lifestyle which is dominated by Christ. So we do not act out a fear of the law of the land, but we act out of a desire to love Jesus and do what pleases him.

One reason why it is so hard for the church to maintain a pure witness in today's world is because many individual believers have been caught in inappropriate sexual behaviour, or in financial impropriety, or in a whole range of other things. When our sinful natures get the better of us we find it difficult as a church to go on witnessing to the saving power of Christ, because who we are as individuals denies the message we preach. That is why I believe that God is calling the church of Jesus in Britain to a far greater level of personal holiness. As the power of the Spirit transforms us and makes us more like the living Christ, so we become more and more the attractive personalities that people long to know. We are to 'live such good lives among the pagans that, though they accuse you of doing wrong, they may see your good deeds and glorify God on the day he visits us' (2:12).

An asset to the community
In order to overcome any accusations, believers have to go on faithfully, not just living a good life internally and having the sinful desires killed, but carry on living good lives externally as well. The Greek word for 'good' in verse 12 means 'beautiful'. Believers should live such beautiful

lives that pagans will be prompted to ask where they got it from.

Christians may well be accused of many negative things by society, but should live such beautiful lives that these accusations are shown for what they are – falsehoods. Instead Christians are to be an asset to their community. That is why Jesus puts such a strong emphasis on caring for the poor, the needy and the helpless, because these are beautiful deeds.

Peter concludes this instruction with the words '[that they may] glorify God *on the day he visits us*'. This phrase is very complicated and interpreters are divided as to its meaning. Some say it is an oblique reference to Peter visiting them, but others, and I think this view is more likely, see it as a reference to God visiting in all his power. They were praying for a revival, just as we are today.

Submission to authority

Peter changes his emphasis at this point and writes about submission: 'Submit yourselves for the Lord's sake to every authority instituted among men: whether to the King, as the supreme authority, or to governors who are sent by him to punish those who do wrong and to commend those who do right' (2:13-14). Most of us have something of the rebel in us and we do not like instruction. We do not want to submit to authority

Some Christians today see the church as completely separate from the state. It is important that we do not possess a negative view of society. The danger is that we look out through the windows of our church buildings and see society as the place where Satan rules. But if we are of the attitude that we will have nothing to do with it, we will never engage the community with the good news of Jesus. They will never know what we are about; they will simply see us as a mysterious group of people who shut ourselves away together for a couple of hours every Sunday. But it is by our good deeds, by our acts of kindness and love, that we will help non-Christians to understand God's love and bring glory and honour to Jesus. This is part of the evangelistic mission task of the church.

and perhaps even feel that we are set apart from worldly authority in the face of the higher authority of God. Sometimes, it is all people can do to be civil to those in authority, especially if they hold opposing political views. But we need to get over that, and pray for authorities both local and national.

For the Lord's sake we are to submit ourselves to human authorities. Their role is 'to punish those who do wrong and to commend those who do right'. Authorities seem to be reasonably good at punishing wrongdoers although they fail at times to understand how to do it, but they are not very good at commending the good and, in fact, much government policy fails to understand this biblical principle. The biblical view of government is that it has the responsibility to punish wrong and commend the good. Our government needs to think carefully about how it commends people who do the right thing, because many people in our society feel penalized for being honest, for living in righteousness and integrity. If it did, society would be a happier place.

Silencing the talk of foolish men

Another reason for doing good is found in verse 15: 'For it is God's will that by doing good you should silence the ignorant talk of foolish men.' These foolish men were very critical of the church. And in our society today it is very easy for the church to be viewed quite negatively. Yet the church generally is condemned on the basis of caricature and rumour, not on the basis of truth. So we have to tell the community what the truth is about the church. In church after church in this country, particularly evangelical and charismatic churches, life and growth are present. It is so important that people form their opinions on the basis of reality and not on the basis of what they think the church is like.

Politicians are desperate to find a moral and

ethical focus in a world where moral values have gone to the wall. They want to see good models of community life and behaviour. What a wonderful opportunity this is for the church to provide a positive model of community for the new millennium. It is vital that we grasp the vision of what we as the church of God can bring to society. We want to invade the world of the arts and science and politics and so on with the good news of Jesus Christ.

Yet we are not to flaunt the freedom we have as believers: 'Live as free men, but do not use your freedom as a cover-up for evil; live as servants of God' (2:16). We are not to be of the opinion that, because Jesus has set us free from the power of sin, we can live in ways that are wrong. Rather we are to live lives that are pure and holy.

Then Peter proceeds to encapsulate the balance of power in terms of our relationship with the state: 'Show proper respect to everyone: Love the brotherhood of believers, fear God, honour the king' (2:17). This balance is vital. Respect for everyone, love for other Christians. We are not to dismiss the state or unbelievers in a cavalier fashion. No, we are to show proper respect, but we do need to recognize the higher priority of love for believers.

And we have to fear God. We have only to *honour* the king, but we have to *fear* God. Our great God is over every king. These first-century believers were hearing of Nero's greatness and were being commanded to honour him, but Peter reminds them that their God is vastly superior. He is the ultimate sovereign, the ultimate king, the ultimate authority.

We are never to be cowed by the authority of the state. It is right for the church to exercise its responsibility, to protest locally and nationally about things we believe to be morally wrong. The state is not to be followed slavishly in that regard. Nevertheless we are not free to disdain the state, we are not free to ignore it, we are not free to forget to pray for it, or for those individuals locally and nationally who represent it. That is the appropriate balance of power between those two relationships. One of the great joys is that we are in a position to model the kind of community which treats the state seriously as a biblically ordained authority structure on the one hand, but to also treat our relationship with God seriously as well.

7

Christians at Work
(2:18-25)

Every chapter of this book considers how Christians are to live successfully in a dangerous world. As Christians we live in a world that does not have Christian values. Therefore a number of appropriate practices have to be put in place to ensure that Christian living does not become substandard.

One of the major themes of Peter's letter is the question of responding to authority. The ultimate authority for Christians is the authority of Jesus Christ. Of course, there are other authorities that we have to acknowledge, although sometimes their authority conflicts with the authority of Jesus. As we saw in the previous chapter, the authority of the state is one such authority. Believers, in general, will obey what the government demands until its demands oppose what Jesus requires. To disobey the Emperor, or one of his officials, would have serious consequences. Still, the Christians were to put Jesus first.

Another area of authority that can cause problems is authority in the workplace, both with regard to those who have authority and those who are under authority. Peter says:

> Slaves, submit yourselves to your masters with all respect, not only to those who are good and considerate, but also to those who are harsh. For it is commendable if a man bears up under the pain of unjust suffering because he is conscious of God. But how is it to your credit if you receive a beating for doing wrong and endure it? But if you suffer for doing good and you endure it, this is commendable before God. To this you were called, because Christ suffered for you, leaving you an example, that you should follow into his steps.
>
> 'He committed no sin, and no deceit was found in his mouth.'
>
> When they hurled their insults at him, he did not retaliate; when he suffered, he made no threats. Instead, he entrusted himself to him who judges justly. He himself bore our sins in his body on the tree, so that we might die to sins and live for righteousness; by his wounds you have been healed. For you were like sheep going astray, but now you have returned to the Shepherd and Overseer of your souls (1 Peter 2:18-25).

Being a slave

It has to be said that this is not an easy passage to transpose straight from the first century into the twentieth century. Most of us, however harsh our employers may be, don't consider ourselves to be slaves. Workers have been given certain rights and for that we should be thankful. But in the first

Peter does not comment about whether slavery itself is right or wrong. Not even Paul does! But what they did do was sow the seeds of the destruction of slavery by redefining the relationship between master and owner. The nearest guidance we have is Paul's letter to Philemon where we find the lovely story of Onesimus, the escaped slave whom Paul is sending back to Philemon. Paul doesn't debate with Philemon about the philosophical right or wrong about having slaves – he sends the slave back. In fact he uses a little joke, because he says Onesimus, whose name means 'useful', had run away and so was 'useless' to Philemon. But now Paul was sending back 'Useless' to be useful to Philemon. The main difference in Onesimus was that after he ran away to Rome, he became a Christian and was useful in helping Paul while he was under house arrest there. What Paul did was to remind Philemon that he owed Paul a great deal because Paul had brought the message of salvation to him. Now Onesimus too had been saved and was returning to his master. Paul exhorts Philemon to treat him as a domestic, if that is his work, but treat him also, at another level, as a brother because Christ has come into both their lives.

century slavery was extremely common. It is calculated that there were almost sixty million slaves in the Roman Empire at that time. That figure is more than the entire population of the United Kingdom today.

Peter does not use the usual Greek word for slavery. Instead he uses a word that means 'domestics', referring to slaves who worked in the homes of wealthy owners. We must not think that slaves were only involved in menial tasks. Many doctors and teachers were slaves. There is evidence that in first century Rome, some of the influential people were slaves. A common practice was for an owner, after realising that a child of one of his slaves was intelligent, to arrange for the child to be educated. But that educated child was still regarded as a slave of his master. So we must not imagine all these slaves being beaten daily and cruelly treated. Some were, of course, but many were not, and some slaves in the Roman Empire were loved and honoured as part of the family.

So Peter is writing to domestic slaves who have become Christians, but whose masters may or may not be believers. What should the attitude of the converted slave be to his owner, and if the owner is a Christian, what should his attitude be to his slaves? These were very important issues in the early church.

And the relationship of Christians to their

employers is obviously important too. Christians have to behave as Christians in the workplace whether or not their boss is a Christian. Sadly, some believers can be a pain to work for and to work with. We can even find ourselves in the workplace with other Christians, and wish for non-Christians to work with because they can be easier to be around.

Sometimes people come and talk to me about working for a Christian organisation, and I discover they would like to do so because they imagine that working in a Christian environment, with a Christian boss and Christian employees, will be like one long prayer meeting and chorus singing exercise. Of course, such an outlook is totally wrong, for sometimes Christian organisations can be harder to work for than non-Christian organisations.

But how do Christians relate to a non-Christian employer or manager? Irrespective of his status in Christian things, believers must behave honourably. Peter gives the example of being beaten unjustly. The type of beating Peter has in mind was given with a clenched fist to the side of the head. He says that if Christians are beaten for bad behaviour, it is no credit to the gospel because they are rightly punished.

When the master was a Christian, there was the temptation for Christian slaves to take advantage of the Christian connection between them. They would meet in the church on the Lord's day, where the slaves could be in positions of leadership; then they would meet back in the workplace and the slaves would be tempted to transfer the relationships in the church to responsibilities in the workplace. Peter says that such behaviour us wrong. Instead, Christian slaves are to submit to their masters with all respect, by giving them the honour due to their position.

Christian slaves were even to show this attitude to masters who were harsh. In our colloquial language we could say that such an employer is 'bent'. And 'bent' would be an accurate translation, for the Greek word *skolios* means a crooked stick, one that is not useful for its task because it is bent. A master who is harsh is so because he is corrupt and twisted, he does not act with honour and integrity. Peter is saying that our response to our employers is not to be in relation to how well they treat us, we are not to let others dictate our behaviour. Many today act in the workplace like petulant children and not like mature adults. If he treats me badly, why should I do what he wants? That would be an immature response for a Christian, and a sinful response. Christians are always to behave in a godly way.

What Peter stresses in this passage is: if you are punished for doing wrong, take it like an adult. But if you are punished for doing right, then glory comes to God if you take it in an honourable way.

Such a response is commendable to God. In fact, when we are involved in undeserved suffering we mirror Jesus. Therefore, it is important to see how Jesus responded to unjust treatment.

Jesus is our example
As I have just said, Peter encourages these Christian slaves by reminding them of the example of Jesus. Some commentators believe that verses 21-25 are a hymn or chorus that was sung by the early church as a summary of their doctrine of Jesus' life and work, a reminder of how Jesus had acted on their behalf. These early Christians endured unjust suffering in the workplace, but what they suffered was nothing compared to the unjust sufferings of Jesus. Suffering is part of their calling, but they fulfil that calling by following in the steps of Christ.

I remember going for a walk with my children across swampy ground. They were quite nervous for they thought they were going to sink into the swamp. So I said, 'I'll go on ahead and look for the more solid bits of ground, and you just step where I have stepped.' They got across relatively wet free because they walked in my steps.

That is the pattern here. Jesus, by walking ahead of us, has given us an example. The word translated 'example' is a very interesting one. It comes from the world of art and architecture. When apprentices were being instructed, the architect or artist would chisel letters into the top of a slate and the apprentice would copy the 'example', and chisel in the exact mirror of the letters underneath. By this process he was learning to craft exactly the same kind of architectural lettering or imagery. Jesus has left us an example of undeserved suffering. Follow precisely the way he lived.

Of course, Jesus is the perfect example: 'he committed no sin and no deceit was found in his mouth.' He never failed. But even the best of Christians make mistakes in the workplace. Even when they flung their insults at him, Jesus did not retaliate. When he suffered, he made no threats. I think Peter is recalling the scene in the Garden of Gethsemene, when Jesus was arrested. There, Peter had used a sword and nearly killed Malchus, the servant of the high priest. But Jesus healed Malchus immediately; neither did he threaten those who had come to arrest him. Instead Jesus 'entrusted himself to him who judges justly'. There is a huge lesson here for us. We are so often tempted to justify ourselves, be it in the workplace, or in the church, or in relationships. We want to say our piece so that people cannot possibly misunderstand where we are coming from. We are often defensive, we are often wanting to establish our rights. Jesus just entrusted himself to the judge of all the earth.

As ordinary Christians, we are going to be

misunderstood in the workplace. Many of us are going to be passed over for promotion. Many of us are going to find ourselves under incredible pressure at various times. We are going to be treated in a way we wish we were not. Sometimes we will never be able to put it right, humanly speaking. But we can entrust ourselves to the One who judges right.

Sometimes Christian leaders are the subject of rumour or of gossip in the church. Whenever I read anything adverse about myself in the Christian press, my initial response is to justify myself by writing to the editor, or by publicly burning the magazine! I want the right of reply. Sometimes I get very frustrated and angry about what people imply or say. Often, in the process of justifying ourselves, we will make the situation worse, because what we perceive as establishing the truth is perceived by others as defensive self-justification. There are times when, like Jesus, leaders have to say, 'I entrust myself to the One who knows my heart. He will judge rightly.'

I have already mentioned that these verses are an early hymn, or else based on a song of praise. It is as if Peter pictures Jesus hanging on the cross. He wanted the Christians to whom he was writing to realise that the penalty of their sins was paid for when Jesus died. But not only did Jesus deal with the penalty of our sins, he also destroyed the power of sin. Our wrong, our twistedness has been straightened out by the Cross, our bentness, our crookedness has been made straight. We have been made clean.

Here Peter is tying theology and practical behaviour. Die to sin, die to self, so that in the workplace we are living to God's agenda. Your employee or your employer will see you living in a completely different way because you are dying to the old life and you are living for righteousness.

Can I ask, 'What are you living for? What dominates your life?' There are many fanatics in our society today, dedicated followers of a wide range of people or beliefs. There are, for example, Islamic Fundamentalists who are so fanatical for their religious observance that some of them are prepared to be suicide bombers. Their focus is clear. We believe it is the wrong focus, but we cannot deny it is passionate and it is life-controlling. To be a Christian fanatic means to have passionate commitment – to live for righteousness, to have it as the focus of life. To live for righteousness means to lives focused on Jesus. And both masters and slaves could do so then, and both employers and employees can do so now.

Peter has a pastor's heart. He realises the difficulty of the challenge he has just given to Christian employers and employees. So to encourage them further he highlights two aspects of the activity of Jesus on their behalf. First, he is the shepherd who cares for his flock, and secondly, he is the overseer who guides and directs the lives of his people.

But what often happens to us, because of the immense pressure in the workplace, is that we can find ourselves drifting away from the Shepherd of our souls and the Overseer of our lives. Instead of keeping close to the Shepherd for protection in his fold, and knowing the guidance of his superior wisdom, we can let our faith grow cold and have no fellowship with him. But if we stay close to the Shepherd, we will experience his care and receive his guidance, and so be able to live for him effectively in the workplace.

8

Christian Marriages
(3:1-7)

Peter has already dealt with the authority of the state and with authority in the workplace, and given principles how Christians are to respond in both situations. The next area of authority that Peter considers is authority in the home.

Wives, in the same way be submissive to your husbands so that, if any of them do not believe the word, they may be won over without words by the behaviour of their wives, when they see the purity and reverence of your lives. Your beauty should not come from outward adornment, such as braided hair and the wearing of gold jewellery and fine clothes. Instead, it should be that of your inner self, the unfading beauty of a gentle and quiet spirit, which is of great worth in God's sight. For this is the way the holy women of the past who put their hope in God used to make themselves beautiful. They were submissive to their own husbands, like Sarah, who obeyed Abraham and called him her master. You are her daughters if you do what is right and do not give way to fear.

Husbands, in the same way be considerate as you live with your wives, and treat them with respect as the weaker partner and as heirs with you of the gracious gift of life, so that nothing will hinder your prayers.

This passage concerning authority in the home is especially challenging today because the question of submission of women to men is a very sensitive subject. Many get hot under the collar over it and discussions of the subject can become heated debates.

As with other passages in 1 Peter it is very important for us to understand why Peter wrote these words. It is a superficial view of the passage to say that it is a male chauvinist charter allowing Christian husbands to claim an unswerving, unquestioning obedience from their wives. So it is essential for us, to begin with, to set Peter's comments in their initial context. Otherwise we will badly misinterpret what he says.

This section of Peter's letter begins at 2:13, and the theme of the section is submission to authority. We saw in previous chapters that Christians, despite being freed by Christ, were to submit to the authority of the state, and that Christian slaves were to submit to the authority of their masters, be they Christians or not. But note that Jesus, too, was submissive – to the will of the Father; this is the primary reason for his coming into the world to die on the cross.

So the teaching regarding a wife's submission to her husband is set in a section that indicates that submission by Christians is required by God, no matter how difficult it might seem. And it is also set in the context of following the example of Christ, who was submissive to God's will despite the personal cost. Christian wives, in fact, are being asked to identify with what Jesus did in his submission to the Father.

Secondly, why is it that in these seven verses, six times as much is said to the women than is said to the men? The reason is this: if we are to live successfully in a dangerous world, we will not only have to cope with relationships in the workplace and with relationships with the state, we will have to develop correct relationships in the home. And, believe it or not, in giving so much more detail to the role of the wife, Peter is showing that Christianity is actually liberating for women.

I need to explain this further. In the cultures of the day, when a man became a Christian, it meant that his wife and family were regarded as Christians as well. This does not mean that they automatically repented and believed, but it did mean that they would automatically be associated with the Christian community. The three cultural backgrounds of the church in the Roman Empire – the Roman, the Greek and the Jewish – all treated women as possessions and not as human beings with personal rights. The only way in the ancient world for women to obtain rights was to marry people with rights. A first century Latin writer said, 'If you catch your wife in a situation which implies immorality, you may kill her without a trial. If she catches you in a similar position you may ignore her response.' In the first century, women were treated extremely badly. They were not perceived as having the ability to make their own decisions. And it is very likely that in the churches to which Peter wrote, there would be wives who had initially become believers, because of the decision of their husbands.

But there were also wives who had become believers without their husbands becoming Christians. As far as the cultures of the time were concerned, these women should not have made that choice. So when a woman made a decision to follow Jesus, a revolution had taken place. Right at the heart of the gospel there is a woman's liberation principle – she could choose to follow Jesus without the approval of her husband, and in that regard she took a step away from the authority of her husband. That is why Christianity was dynamite in the ancient world, it was seen as a threat to the male-dominated order.

Christianity did not deny that a wife should have strong allegiance to her husband, but it also affirmed that there is a higher authority than the husband, that is, Jesus Christ. And it affirmed that it was possible for a woman in her own right to choose to follow Jesus as her Saviour and Lord, despite the religion her husband may have chosen to follow. And as today, in the churches then there were many women without their husbands. And it is to address that practical question – how could Christian women win their non-Christian partners to Jesus Christ? – that Peter writes this passage. He makes it clear it will not be easy. But he does give several important principles to help wives with non-Christian husbands. So what at first sight seems a crushing demand on women is actually going to be their releasing, and gives them the opportunity of being involved in winning their husbands for Jesus.

Characteristics of Christian wives
The first characteristic of Christian wives is *submission to their husbands* (3:1-2). The word 'submissive' can be misunderstood, because we can use it aggressively. When I was young I associated the word with wrestling, to the moment when one of the wrestlers forced the other to submit out of desperation and pain. And, sadly, submission is often seen by Christians with the sense of crushing, bullying, the giving way under incredible pressure. But biblical submission is not something that someone imposes on you, it is something you take on board yourself. Peter is not telling husbands to bully and crush their wives into submission, rather he is urging the wives to voluntarily take on the role of being willing to submit to their husbands.

Peter explains why this attitude of submission is so important. By being submissive to her unconverted husband a Christian wife may win him for Jesus by the beauty of her life. (As an aside, but a very important one, I would encourage you to pray intelligently for Christian ladies whose husbands are not believers. What we must pray for, perhaps above everything, is for these ladies to be given real strength to live lives of voluntary selflessness.)

The second characteristic of Christian wives should be *spiritual beauty*. In verses 3 and 4 Peter describes it. Their beauty is not dependant on outward adornments such as braided hair and the wearing of gold jewellery and fine clothes. Peter is not saying that a woman should not look beautiful or dress well. Rather, what he is saying is this: a woman who wants to win her husband to Christ, by being the woman God wants her to be, will not rely on external adornments. True beauty is voluntary selflessness, purity and reverence. It comes from an inner walk with God.

This emphasis of Peter's is very relevant for today. We live in a culture that is obsessed with external adornments, that is body obsessed. And our culture can force us to focus on the external. So Peter is telling Christian wives to be careful that they don't buy into the prevailing culture. Their ultimate beauty to God is a far deeper, far less superficial, thing. It is far more important that they are at their hearts, beautiful people.

The unfading beauty of a gentle and quiet spirit is of great worth in the sight of God (verse 4). And Peter uses as an example Sarah, the wife of Abraham, who obeyed him and 'called him her master'. Even her speech was marked by respect for her husband.

Characteristics of Christian husbands
Peter mentions three features of a godly husband: they are to be considerate of their wives, they are to respect their wives even although they are physically weaker, and they are to realize that their wives are just as much heirs of grace as they are.

'Considerate' is a difficult word to translate, it means treat your wife 'according to knowledge'. Since the word 'know' is used in the Bible with a sexual connotation I would suggest that 'according to knowledge' simply means 'in your dealings with your wife sexually'. So the basic meaning is 'be considerate in your sexual dealings with your wife'. This was revolutionary teaching, for in the ancient world a man had sex with his wife when he wanted it. The thought that she might have a view on the subject never occurred to him. What Peter is saying here is that in sexual relations husbands are to be considerate of the needs of their wives.

But the husband is also to treat his wife with respect. The idea behind the word translated 'respect' is 'precious'. It is found, for example, in 1 Peter 2:6 where Peter, talking of Jesus, says: 'See I lay a stone in Zion, a chosen and precious corner stone.' So husbands, treat your wives as precious, honour them and value them. How easy it is for Christian husbands to treat their wives with neglect, with arrogance, with condescension or even with oblivion. Husbands so often take their wives for granted. They forget what a precious gift they are from God. Although they are physically weaker, they are joint heirs of God with their husbands. Both will share in the treasure of eternity and enjoy it forever.

Then Peter gives this solemn warning to husbands: if they do not treat their wives well, their prayer life will be ineffective. Husbands cannot expect God to accept their prayers and love and worship if in fact, in the home, they are living lives which displease God. So this is a word of warning. We need to be careful in the way we deal with one another in our families so that our prayers can have full reign and there is no blockage and God can burst through.

9

Trouble in the Church
(3:8-12)

In the verses we will reflect on in this chapter Peter considers trouble that can come to believers from within the church, whereas in the verse we shall look at in the next chapter describes persecution from outside the church.

> Finally, all of you, live in harmony with one another; be sympathetic, love as brothers, be compassionate and humble. Do not repay evil or insult with insult, but with blessing, because to this you were called so that you may inherit a blessing. For,
>
> 'Whoever would love life and see good days must keep his tongue from evil and his lips from deceitful speech. He must turn from evil and do good; he must seek peace and pursue it. For the eyes of the Lord are on the righteous and his ears are attentive to their prayer, but the face of the Lord is against those who do evil.'

We need to remember that Peter's original readers had only been Christians for a short time and therefore still had lots of rough edges which affected their relationships with one another.

Churches can inflict pain upon its members; in fact, sometimes, churches can be very cruel. I often speak to ministers' fraternals and leadership gatherings and am always amazed at the number of ministers who have been damaged by the way they have been treated by their congregations. But I also speak to congregations who have been most damaged, not by their contact with a non-Christian world, but by their pastor or leaders.

So how are these problems to be sorted out? Peter mentions five ways in these verses:

live in harmony with one another,
be sympathetic,
love as brothers,
be compassionate
be humble.

Live in harmony

'Live in harmony with one another' translates one Greek word which means 'like-minded'. So to live in harmony with one another means to 'mind' the same things, to think in the same way. But this is not a call for harmony by cloning. The Bible does not expect believers to stop thinking for themselves, and there are plenty issues on which Christians can disagree without any view being wrong. What is looked for in the life of the church is unanimity not uniformity, and that is a very important principle to understand. If we look for uniformity we will be trying to clone one another and will be like-minded in the wrong sense. Uniformity means everybody has to think in the same way about every aspect of Christian doctrine and living. Unanimity, on the other hand, is seen when our minds are focused on the things of God because we love him and delight to meet with him. In these encounters with God our minds are being renewed, and the evidence of continual renewal is that we want the best for the people of God, that we long to see his Word known and loved among them, that we long to see his Kingdom come in power, and we long that the world will believe in the name of Jesus. Unanimity means that we are absorbed with the same vision, are like-minded in terms of the overall vision. That's why mission statements can be so helpful for churches because they focus the mind of the church corporately on similar goals and agendas. We are not to be distracted over trivia and detail and minutiae.

An illustration may help you understand what I mean. When a mother is trying to discipline her children, and the grandmother is also present, the grandmother may say to the children, 'Mind your mother.' In other words, Do what she is telling you to do. So if we are to be like-minded, we are to mind our Father. Christians have different gifts, different interests, different temperaments, but as we are like-minded with God and seek his mind, and follow him, so our church will experience unanimity within a great creative diversity. So we are to be like-minded, absorbed with what God wants, and ready to do his will.

Be sympathetic

Actually, the literal translation of these words is 'suffer with'. Christians are to suffer with those who hurt. We are to engage with those who are in pain. When one member of the body hurts, all the members of the body hurt; and when one rejoices, all the members of the body rejoice. When something hurtful happens to others of God's people, we feel with them because we are bound together in the body of Christ. When this happens, it is strong evidence of the wonderful work of the Spirit in the congregation. For example, a Christian may pray to be healed, but God says 'No'. But when that person rejoices at the healing of another believer, and when the healed believer suffers with the one who was not healed, that's the power of the Spirit working in their lives. They are really experiencing what body life is all about.

Love as brothers

Many of you will know that Philadelphia, one of the great cities of America, means 'the city of brotherly love'. In Greek there are several words for 'love' and the noun *phileo,* used here, does not mean an erotic, sexual love, nor does it mean a paternal or maternal love, nor does it even mean *agape* love. It means a brotherly, sisterly love and concern for one another. I do not want to imply that *phileo* love is inferior to *agape* love. I suspect that the New Testament uses the rich variety of Greek terminology regarding love to bring out its essential features for church life, as well as God's love for us. 1 Corinthians 13 summarises this deep love Christians should have for one another. What is absolutely essential in the life of a church is not just to be like-minded, nor is it merely to have sympathy, wonderful though that is, but to love with that wonderful love the Holy Spirit sheds abroad in our hearts. Almost all the problems in the lives of local churches can be dealt with when there is a baptism of love on the people of God as a whole.

Be compassionate

Compassion, the fourth emphasis, is love in action. I can remember being startled, some years ago, reading reports from a number of relief organisations in which they used the same phrase, a phrase that was both frightening and revealing. They said that, because so much had been seen on our TV screens about suffering in the Third World, the nation was suffering from 'compassion fatigue'. How sad it is to come to a situation where we do not respond any more. The first century was a suffering world for many people, including many Christians, and Peter realised there was a danger of compassion fatigue.

Christians might see someone in great need, and may even offer an hour of prayer for them, but to actually put love into practice and do something about it is very rare indeed. The great thing about compassion is that it is an activity; it means looking round and when it sees people in need, in love it does something about it. It can be as elementary as taking a meal to someone, or it might be a telephone call or a letter expressing love. Compassion is the involvement of love practically in peoples' lives.

The reason why Christians find compassion to be hard is because they do not see with the eyes of Christ. The word translated 'compassion' literally means 'guts', the internal organs. Often the King James Version translates 'compassion' as 'bowels of mercy'. We have to learn to have such a deep concern for one another that we see beyond the superficial response.

Quite a few lies are told every time Christians meet together. 'How are you, today?' 'Fine!' That type of greeting is just a kind of verbal wallpaper, just background noise. We need to get beyond that and discover where those we are speaking to are and what they need at that time. If compassion is be real, we will listen beyond those trivial and superficial things.

Edgar Hoover was once at a reception line with the President of the USA, and people kept passing, without listening to what was being said, but instead being very ingratiating, saying 'How nice to see you' and so on. Hoover was fed up with the superficiality. And so to every person who passed him he said, 'I killed my wife's mother last night!' And all they said was, 'Nice to see you.' Nobody said anything different until one ambassador from a foreign country, as he bowed to him, replied, 'The old bat deserved it!'

I don't think Christians are listening to each other. That is because we are not listening to God. God calls us to be filled with love and compassionate. Something deep within us should respond to the need in others, we must go beyond the superficial into the deep needs of people. We cannot care for everybody, but we can reach out in love to the one or two we are in contact with each week.

Be humble
The fifth requirement is a call to be humble. Humility is a very strategic but simple outlook that it is vital in the life of the church. If we are to take on the mantle of our Master, Philippians 2 makes it clear that Jesus was the one who did not count equality with God a thing to be grasped, but made himself of no reputation and humbled himself to death, even death on a cross. So as we live in the light of our Master's character we will humble ourselves before him and will be humble

in our dealings with one another. In the church of Jesus, an arrogant self centredness is entirely out of place.

So if you want to be someone who avoids suffering in the church and avoids creating it for others, live in those five ways of being like-minded, sympathetic, exercising brotherly love, compassionate and humble.

Being a realistic leader, Peter knew that Christians do not always practice these five requirements and are often faced with the situation of having to respond to evil attitudes and behaviour in the church. Therefore, he adds: 'Don't repay evil with evil, or insult with insult but with blessing, because to this you were called so that you may inherit a blessing.' We can almost hear the words of Jesus from his teaching in the Sermon on the Mount in this verse from Peter. Christians are to bring blessing even when they are in pain.

In the early church there were different groupings based on social levels (such as masters and slaves) or different racial backgrounds. It is not difficult to imagine that there could be an element of distrust in a church, particularly between masters and slaves. In the life of the church, if resentments breed, insults will lead to bitterness. And if such differences are allowed to continue, it will be hard to break down the barriers between the various groupings.

How does a Christian get even with those who have damaged him in the life of the church? By blessing them! We bless them because of the blessing we have inherited from Jesus Christ – and that we are going to go on inheriting. This is another example of the turn the other cheek ministry of Jesus. When someone strikes you on one cheek, turn the another. This attitude can only be there if we have died to selfishness. Then if we are insulted, we will be mature enough in the things of God, not to repay it with an insult, but to repay it with love. In theory, the ruder and more destructive and negative you are towards me, the more loving I should be towards to you.

There is no question that the Bible makes it absolutely clear that the standard policy for Christians is for each of them not to allow resentments to fester when they are hurt or damaged. Now this philosophy has been rejected by many of the great philosophers of the world who have seen it as one of the great weaknesses of Christianity. Nietsche, in the 1930s, wrote about the teaching of Jesus about turning the other face and said: 'We are not so weak as to live as the Christians do, but we return fist for even bigger fist.' He made it absolutely clear that, in his view, the master race will be those who take no nonsense from anybody, and power is met with an even greater power. That is not the way of the Christian. The way of the Christian is to imitate Jesus – the

Jesus who conquered by suffering. He was the Servant King who gave his life for us.

What a great thing it is to bless other people. This is not referring to a simple blessing, such as saying 'God bless you' to everybody. Of course, there is something warm and reassuring when a fellow Christian puts their arm around you and says, 'God bless you!' But Peter is referring to practical blessing, to reaching out and doing something, by blessing with an action of some kind.

Of course, we all know how hard it is to have this attitude. Sinful human nature sees blessing those who offend us as the last thing to do. That is why Christians need the baptism and the power of the Holy Spirit in order to be different from what sinful humans do, and instead to be like Jesus. Peter quotes from Isaiah 53 to show what Jesus did when he was maliciously insulted: 'Like a sheep before its shearers is dumb, he opened not his mouth.' The Son of God was insulted by Herod and Pilot. He had the power to wipe them off the face of the earth, but he choose not to.

Then Peter quotes from Psalm 34: 'Whoever would love life and see good days, must keep his tongue from evil, and his lips from deceitful speech.' If we are going to avoid suffering in the life of the church we are going to have to watch our mouths. Our tongue can be a devastating weapon of Satan inside our church. I am very impressed with the Old Testament incident of live coals being placed on the lips of the prophet Isaiah (Isaiah 6). Our lips need to be burned by the hot coals of the divine presence. We need to stop gossiping, lying and deceitful talk. Instead, we need holy lips to speak out far more readily the truth of the Word of God in witness and evangelism. May our lips be so cauterised by the Holy Spirit that we can only speak purity, holiness, encouragement and upbuilding. Let us commit ourselves to only use our lips to build up others, to bless others, to share the good news of Jesus with others.

Every Christian must 'seek peace and pursue it'. Again this parallels what Jesus said in the Sermon on the Mount: 'Blessed are the peacemakers.' Peter urges each believer to be an agent of reconciliation, to be a mediator. This a very important role in the life of the church, because people do fall out because of personality clashes and misunderstandings in communication. A peacemaker looks for every opportunity to bring harmony between two fighting and struggling individuals or different viewpoints. He will not do it at the expense of truth, but with truth as a backdrop. He will explaining more of what we have in common as the people of God.

Peter, continuing to quote from the psalmist, says why these correct attitudes are important: 'For the eyes of the Lord are on the righteous and his ears are attentive to their prayer, but the face of the Lord is against those who do evil.' His eyes are on us, he sees where we are, and he listens out for us. His ears are attentive to our prayer. If we do things that displease him God will actively oppose us. But when we are co-operating with him, and our lives are filled with harmony, sympathy, love, compassion and humility, when we are blessing others, when our lips are speaking holiness and not condemnation, when we are pursuing peace as agents of reconciliation, he is pleased with us.

10

Anticipating Persecution
(3:13-17)

Although the New International Version begins verse 13 with 'who', in the original the first word is 'and', obviously linking verse 13 to verse 12:

> 'Who is going to harm you, if you are eager to do good? But even if you should suffer for what is right, you are blessed. "Do not fear what they fear, do not be frightened." But in your hearts set apart Christ as Lord. Always be prepared to give an answer to everyone who asks you to give the reason for the hope that you have. But do this with gentleness and respect, keeping a clear conscience, so that those who speak maliciously against your good behaviour in Christ may be ashamed of their slander. It is better, if it is God's will, to suffer for doing good than for doing evil.

In Peter's day the threat of persecution was ever present. It may be the case that his readers were not being persecuted at that precise moment, but they had been in the past and would be again in the future. Now that is a very tense situation in which to live. If you are coping with persecution, that is one thing, at least you know what you are facing. Again, if there is no persecution at all, then

The twentieth century has actually seen more Christians martyred for their faith than the previous nineteen centuries combined. So persecution in the world today is not an abstract theoretical concept, it is happening now in many parts of the world.

the matter is settled. But to be living in this very pressurised, explosive situation, where at any moment persecution could become real, is very difficult. So to struggling believers, Peter lists six principles that will help them live in a world where persecution was likely: don't be afraid, put Jesus first, defend the faith, be considerate, have a clear conscience and go on going good.

Peter says that we are *not to be afraid* because the eyes of the Lord are upon us (verse 12). And he asks them to consider, 'Who will harm you for doing good?' This question raises the role of the magistrate in the first century, which was that he was not to harm those who lived good lives. So, in general, Christians were not to be afraid of the authorities, although at times they may be punished wrongly for doing good; but in the main, if they continued living good lives, the secular world would either leave them alone or would affirm their good deeds. The same call comes to us today as believers. Although we are a minority in our society, we are not to be afraid because the eyes of the Lord are upon us. If we are doing good, he will affirm us as we live righteous lives.

Yet suffering and Christianity are not alternatives. And I think it is important to mention here that neither is there always a connection between suffering and sin. Some believers go through horrendous experiences of guilt because they imagine that God is punishing them. They come in pain for pastoral counselling and say, 'I feel dreadful and wretched. What have I done wrong?' And they have to be reassured that they are not suffering because of a sin.

Peter is not encouraging an unhealthy masochism about suffering. Christians are not to want suffering. But when it happens, we are to realise that suffering is shaping our spirituality, that it is maturing our personality. Suffering is meant to drive us back into the arms of God.

Therefore, Peter tells his readers to react differently from the way non-Christians do when they are in trouble: 'So do not fear what they fear,' in other words, do not be terrified by what people in the world are terrified by. 'Fear not' is the great motif throughout the teaching of Jesus. He was constantly saying it to his band of disciples who were repeatedly falling apart around him. There was Thomas, a sort of perpetual cynic, a perpetual doubter about everything. There was Peter, who made all sorts of statements and then regretted them. There were James and John, who wanted to call fire down from heaven on the Samaritans who refused hospitality to Jesus. Jesus had constantly to tell them: 'Look, stop worrying. I am constantly with you. Do not be afraid.'

Perhaps the most striking incidence of this is the lovely episode on the lake. Although there is a great storm, Jesus is asleep in the boat. The disciples waken him and say, 'Master, don't you care that we are dying?' 'Don't be afraid,' Jesus said to them. Now that seems a slightly odd thing to say. If I was in the middle of Lake Galilee in a tremendous storm and the boat was taking in water, and someone said to me, 'Don't be afraid!' I would suspect that he was not facing reality. However, the words of Jesus about not being afraid are not some slick panacea, but indicate he is intending to do a deep, permanent work in their hearts and minds. We are not to be frightened because our destiny is ultimately not in our hands, nor in the hands of those politicians who believe they enact our destiny, nor in the brains of economists who believe they can predict our destiny, nor in the theories of social scientists who believe they can control our destiny, nor in the programmes of educators who believe they can prepare us for our destiny. Our destiny ultimately lies in the hands of the One who rules the universe. We are his people, therefore we are not to be afraid. Of course, we need the Holy Spirit to produce this attitude, otherwise what we are working up is only human willpower.

God can deliver us from many of the fears with which we live and set us free to be the men and women that he wants us to be. He wants us to be encouraged in a world where fear reigns, be it fear of the future, or fear of the past, or fear of the present. This God speaks to us from 1 Peter saying, 'Do not be afraid.' For some reading this, it may be that this simple reminder from Peter will be the word of encouragement that you need, as you face a situation that perhaps nobody else knows about. But God can give you his peace.

Instead of being afraid, Christians are to *in their hearts set apart Jesus as Lord*. The part of our being described as 'heart' refers to the core of one's being. The New Testament does not tend to use the word 'heart' as we would use it – as describing our emotions. Rather, it refers to the centre of who each of us really is, and there each of us is to set apart Christ as Lord.

Peter identifies the Jesus who walked with him on earth as the Lord of the Universe. When the New Testament uses the word 'Lord' with reference to Jesus, it is usually translating the Greek rendering of the Old Testament name for God – 'Yahweh' or 'I am'. A number of commentators have said that this verse is the clearest statement by Peter of the divinity of Jesus. Jesus, for Peter, is not simply a human leader to be followed, a good act to get involved in, a hero to emulate. No, he is the Lord. So if you are fearful about being persecuted, then put Jesus first in your life, set him apart as Lord

So we follow Jesus by giving him our allegiance. He is to have total control in our lives, we are to do what he says, to be dictated to by his purposes, to be led by his will, to live for his cause. To be obedient to him is probably the single greatest thing a believer can do.

In addition to setting Christ apart as Lord in our hearts, we are to 'always be prepared to give an answer to everyone who asks you to give the reason for the hope that you have'. Christians are to be always ready to defend the faith. The Greek word translated as 'giving a reason' is the one from which we get the English word 'apology' (in a technical sense, not in the sense of saying sorry for a mistake). The implications of the original language is that Peter has in mind the formal setting of a law court. He urges his fellow Christians to prepare for the possibility of being tried for being a Christian. But he is also thinking about informal settings, because he refers to 'everyone who asks you'. No doubt Peter often remembered the time when he denied his Master three times during an informal setting. But after Pentecost a different Peter appears; before the Sanhedrin, the highest Jewish court, he testified courageously regarding Jesus. He stood before them in the power of the Spirit, ready to give a defence of his faith.

This courageous witness is seen throughout the Acts of the Apostles. Stephen constantly reasoned with the Jewish leaders, and his God-given courage is especially seen in the address he gave just before his martyrdom. What he said was a rational, reasonable defence of why Jesus had come. Similarly, Paul on the Areopagus, when speaking to the philosophers of Athens, gave a step by step unfolding of the purposes of God.

All Christians should be able to give a reason for the hope that they have. There are some very good books available on popular apologetics. They can help us answer some of the difficult questions that people may ask us. Of course, the questions will be different to the questions faced in the first century. But why are we Christians? Do we know what and why we believe? It is important for us to know why we believe, and what we believe. We may have to work hard at thinking through the reasons for our faith, but it will be worth it if we are then able to articulate what we believe.

Today, people do not have a big picture of reality (meta-narrative is the technical term). Instead, in our post-modern western world, everyone believes that everything they believe is as true as anything anybody else believes. Everyone has their own little picture, their own understanding of what is truth. Christians have a massive task in convincing others that there is universal truth, that there is a big picture revealed by God in the Bible. How wonderful it is that God will help us in this task.

The Christian method of communicating truth to men and women, who have no experience of this faith, is do it with humility and gentleness, and not arrogance that implies they are fools for having their outlooks. If we are not considerate, the way we speak denies the truth of the gospel we proclaim. Do it, says Peter, with *gentleness and respect*.

At the same time, Christians need to *keep a clear conscience*, in order to give a credible witness. When we have a clear conscience, those who speak maliciously against our good behaviour are going to be ashamed in the long term. That does not mean that they are going to *feel* ashamed, it means that it will be obvious to everybody that their actions are not appropriate and that we are doing the right thing. Sometimes when we are criticised we just have to go on doing the right thing until eventually, sometimes after months or even years, the goodness and rightness of what we do surfaces against all the odds. So keep on doing good.

Far too many Christians are motivated by their emotions and so if they are feeling good about one another and about Jesus, they do good things. But if they feel bad about their relationship with God, or if they are struggling or their circumstances are adverse, then they don't do good things. Whereas our motivation should be to do the right thing, however we feel.

The danger facing those to whom Peter was writing was for them to retreat into a shell and do nothing because of the probability of persecution. But Peter urges them to continue to live radically different lives so that non-Christians will ask concerning their faith. Whatever their reaction may be, if believers continued to live in righteous ways, in the end they would be vindicated.

11

Remember What God Has Done
(3:18-22)

In verses 18-20 Peter says, Remember what God has done in the past – his acts in history, and then in verses 21 and 22 he draws attention to what God is doing in the present.

> For Christ died for sins once for all, the righteous for the unrighteous, to bring you to God. He was put to death in the body but made alive by the Spirit, through whom also he went and preached to the spirits in prison who disobeyed long ago when God waited patiently in the days of Noah while the ark was being built. In it only a few people, eight in all, were saved through water, and this water symbolises baptism that now saves you also – not the removal of dirt from the body but the pledge of a good conscience towards God. It saves you by the resurrection of Jesus Christ, who has gone into heaven and is at God's right hand – with angels, authorities and powers in submission to him.

The death of Christ
To begin with, I will explain some of the technicalities of verse 18 and then I will apply it to our situation.

(1) The word 'Christ' is the New Testament equivalent of the Old Testament word Messiah, meaning 'the anointed one' or 'the sent one'.

(2) Jesus died for sins 'once for all' which means there is no need to repeat his work. The suffering that Jesus went through was on behalf of all of humanity, without exception and without distinction. All of humanity has been made available to God, in other words we can all respond to this message because of what Jesus has done.

(3) Peter describes Jesus as 'the righteous'. It means that Jesus did not do anything wrong. Although he was condemned to die a criminal's death, he had never sinned.

(4) Jesus was made alive by the Spirit. Jesus arose from the dead and is alive for ever. This is an immensely exciting truth for Christians. It means that for them death is not a terminus, but simply the place where we change platforms to go on to another destination.

When you are struggling and things are difficult, remind yourself that Jesus died for you to take away your sin. All your guilt and dirt is gone. And if you are going through suffering, remember too that Jesus rose for you and death is not the end for you. Even if you suffer unto death, no one can take away the treasure that God has placed in your heart. One cannot destroy a Christian, death simply transfers him to heaven.

Victory

But what does verses 19 and 20 mean: 'through whom also he went and preached to the spirits in prison who disobeyed long ago when God waited patiently in the days of Noah while the ark was being built.' Martin Luther commented on this verse: 'A wonderful text is this and a more obscure passage perhaps than any other in the New Testament. So that I do not know for a certainty just what Peter means.' That is very helpful! But to be fair to Luther, not even John Calvin knew what it meant, and almost every Bible scholar since has not known what it means for certain.

Although this is an immensely complicated passage, there are two comments that may help us. First, Peter writes it in the context of assurance about suffering, therefore it must mean something good since Peter's aim is to encourage God's suffering people. Secondly, the people to whom he wrote must have understood it, otherwise there is no point in his referring to it. Having said that, there is still a great deal of disagreement between evangelical Christian scholars about what these verses are describing. There are three major explanations. Let me tell you the first two and then the truth!

Firstly, some say that Peter is indicating that Jesus, between his death and resurrection, preached to those people who perished in the time of Noah. One obvious problem with this

117

interpretation is that it appears to support the possibility of a another opportunity for unbelievers, after death, to respond to God's grace.

The second explanation is that the Spirit of Christ was in Noah when Noah was preaching to these people about the coming flood. Again I find this explanation difficult, because I cannot see what sort of comfort that would have been to people in suffering.

The third explanation, which I tentatively share, is that Jesus did what the Creed says, he descended into Hell or Hades, and there that he actually preached to evil spirits, those rebellious demonic forces who had disobeyed long ago at the time of the flood. He declared to the powers of darkness that he was Lord and that their destiny is sealed. That would be a great encouragement to the people of Peter's day because they were aware of so much demonic activity, those dark powers that influenced what went on in the world. It is very encouraging to know that Christ has and will triumph over evil.

God calls us into this glorious knowledge that, because of the death and resurrection of Jesus, the dark powers are held in their place and we can have victory. Because of Jesus being in control, our churches can make a difference in our communities.

Baptism

But Peter does not only refer to what God has done in the past, he also considers what God is doing in the present. He writes that what happened to Noah and his family, when they were preserved in the ark from drowning, is a picture of *baptism*. Baptism is so important for Christians because it symbolises what God has already done when he cleansed us from sin and what he continues to do – cleansing us from sin.

Baptism is the pledge of a good conscience toward God. The word 'pledge' is a business term that means one has agreed to a contract. So when you were baptised, a contract was exchanged, and you were given a good conscience by God because he had cleaned you up on the inside. Baptism assures us that God will continue being with us through all of our lives. We are being cleaned up on the inside, as the Holy Spirit is working within us. In those dark days when I can't feel God, and he seems a million miles away, the reality is that he is still working inside of me because of my baptism.

12

Live Differently
(1 Peter 4:1-5)

In this chapter, I want us to think in a positive way about how we are going to live for God in this dangerous world – not simply cope with the suffering but living positively for him. Peter gives us teaching on how to do so in 1 Peter 4:1-5:

> Therefore, since Christ suffered in his body, arm yourselves also with the same attitude, because he who has suffered in his body is done with sin. As a result, he does not live the rest of his earthly life for evil human desires, but rather for the will of God. For you have spent enough time in the past doing what pagans choose to do – living in debauchery, lust, drunkenness, orgies, carousing and detestable idolatry. They think it strange that you do not plunge with them into the same flood of dissipation, and they heap abuse on you. But they will have to give account to him who is ready to judge the living and the dead.

How are we to live for God in a dangerous world? First century believers were constantly asking themselves that question. For them, it was not a question for idle speculation, because they were

120

under immense pressure. They didn't just have endless house group meetings, sitting around asking, 'Oh, I wonder how I might live for God?'

There is nothing theoretical or abstract about this passage. It is about practical living for Jesus. It was worked out in the lives of first-century Christians and it must be worked out by us. Yet it is surrounded by the theological truth of the death of Jesus: note Peter's emphasis on 'since Christ suffered in his body'. All he is going to say about Christian living is based on the fact the Jesus suffered in his body. It is interesting that the Bible appeals to the death of Jesus as a comfort to those who are going through suffering.

Jesus really suffered in his body. His death was not a pretence. Although Jesus was God his death was not less painful or less traumatic than the death of other human beings. Jesus suffered in his body just like anybody else would suffer. Therefore, believers are to arm themselves with the same attitude that Jesus had. The attitude of Jesus is unpacked in Philippians 2:5-11, the attitude of humble willingness to submit to the will of God. When we do that we will view suffering, not as an enemy to be avoided, but a friend bringing spiritual maturity.

Peter comments that those who suffer *are done with sin* (verse 1). He does not mean that Christians are sinless. Rather, having to suffer for the faith indicates that they no longer live sinful lives, and it is in that sense of practical living that they are done with sin Their new way of living is out of gratitude to Jesus for what he did on the cross and they commit themselves to not let sin dominate their lives, but instead determine to live according to the will of God.

Now the will of God is a biblical concept which is generally confused with guidance. We have all met believers who are always trying to find the will of God for every detail of their lives. But the will of God in the Bible is the general revelation of the purposes of God in terms of his moral teaching and spiritual demands, not the detailed guidance which some of us seem to want from him.

Augustine was correct in his understanding of the will of God. He said that the question of guidance is simply a matter of loving God and doing what you want. Those believers who neurotically seek God about every detail do not allow themselves to be treated like sons of God; instead they want to be robots. But the Bible constantly forces us on to maturity.

God has revealed his general will in the Scriptures. For example, if you are struggling with gossip, there is no need to pray for guidance about what to do. Just stop gossiping, for it is clear what God's will is. But when we find ourselves in situations where we do not know what to do, we consult our heavenly Father and he gladly gives us wisdom to operate with the freedom that he gives his children. For remember, he has set us free from rules and regulations. I am not suggesting we should not pray about events in our life, of course we should. But I am encouraging you to have the freedom to live in his presence knowing that the boundaries around our lives are the whole of scripture.

Christians have to live for God in a pagan environment that is marked by sinful practices which Peter proceeds to highlight (verse 2). There are three areas in particular that Peter mentions: sexual immorality, alcohol abuse and idolatry. Peter describes the society of the first century very graphically and accurately. And it is an accurate description of the world in which we live. Christians say no to that types of living because they are not part of the will of God. Yet, because they too lived that way before becoming believers, they know that God is able to deliver people from those kinds of lifestyles.

The Bible's teaching on sexuality is very clear: believers must engage in chastity outside marriage and faithfulness inside marriage. But its teaching on sexuality is not negative, but immensely positive. Read the Song of Solomon, a classic example of the Bible's rich vein of teaching in terms of romantic love and sexuality.

The Bible is also clear in its teaching on alcohol. Drunkenness, or anything approaching it, is inappropriate behaviour for the Christian. But the Bible does not condemn the drinking of alcohol. Yet we must remember that we live in a society where many problems are alcohol related, and it may be the most effective witness for Christians to abstain from alcohol.

The third area condemned by Peter is idolatry. Now, Christians don't participate in the worship of idols. Yet we can have many other objects or aims that are as idolatrous as worshipping pagan images. Our form of idolatry can be status or success. In fact, anything that takes the place of Jesus is an idol.

Of course, the pagans will think it strange that Christians do not join them in their sinful living (verse 4). Standing out for Jesus will ultimately cause unbelievers to bring pressure on Christians to conform. They find Christians difficult because they are marching to the beat of a different drummer. The pounding beat of God's relentless love guides us to serve him. But we are out of step with the world, and when one is out of step in a march it looks odd. That is why there were so many martyrs in the first century. They refused to march to the beat of 'Caesar is Lord', and so were put to death. Now we are unlikely to be faced with that kind of dramatic choice, but Peter makes it quite clear that we are going to have to resist society's pressure, because if we do not resist it, we will be the same as they are, conforming to all their values and standards. May God give us the power to resist the pressure from society.

Peter reminds his readers that those who live sinful lives will yet be judged by God (verse 5). All the world will be called to account by him. I find that tremendously reassuring. Every one who ever lived, including those who trouble or persecute his people, are going to bow the knee to Jesus and acknowledge that he is Lord and the judge of all the world.

13

Love in Action
(1 Peter 4:7-11)

The end of all things is near. Therefore be clear
minded and self-controlled so that you can pray.
Above all, love each other deeply, because love
covers over a multitude of sins. Offer hospitality
to one another without grumbling. Each one should
use whatever gift he has received to serve others,
faithfully administering God's grace in its various
forms. If anyone speaks, he should do it as one
speaking the very words of God. If anyone serves,
he should do it with the strength God provides, so
that in all things God may be praised through Jesus
Christ. To him be the glory and the power for ever
and ever. Amen.

This section begins with a very practical
affirmation: 'The end of all things is near.' The
word 'near' urges readiness on behalf of the
readers. Remember that in the first century,
believers were surrounded by enemy forces. One
enemy was the Roman government which was
beginning to regard the fledgling Church as
insurrectionist and threatening. Christians found
themselves oppressed and threatened. Living
under the threat of persecution, they were glad to

In 1 Peter 4:6 Peter refers to certain people in an unusual way: 'the gospel was preached even to those who are now dead.' To whom is he referring and what does he mean? Remember Peter is writing to second generation Christians, and it is certainly the case that some of the first generation of Christians would have died and gone to be with the Lord. They had heard the gospel and believed in Jesus. Critics of Christianity would have concluded that it was a false message because some of those who received Jesus as Saviour had died. 'Where is the evidence of eternal life?' they asked.

Peter's response is to point out that such critics are viewing things from a human point of view only. If the Christians view things from a divine point of view, they will see that the dead believers are still alive. Although their bodies are dead, the eternal life that they had been given when they trusted in Christ remains, as far as their spirits are concerned. They are living in heaven, in the very presence of God.

So we must make a judgement, not on the basis of what we see with our human eyes, but on the basis of what God says.

know that the second coming of Jesus was something they could anticipate.

Some critics use this statement of Peter's as proof of errors in the Bible, for almost 2,000 years have passed since Peter wrote these words, and

Jesus has not returned. But the fact of the matter is that Peter did not know when the second coming was to happen, any more that you or I do. The Bible encourages us not to speculate on the actual timing, but rather to live each day in the expectation of Jesus' coming. The coming of Jesus may be in my lifetime – it may not. But what matters is that I live with the joyful expectation that one day he will return.

Because Jesus is coming, believers are to be *clear minded and self controlled*. The word 'clear mindedness' was used in the first century by the forerunners of the psychologist and the psychiatrist of today. Literally, it means 'sane'. Believers were not to let their minds be disturbed by strange ideas. And 'self control' is the opposite of being controlled by something else, for example, when a person is drunk, he is not in control of himself.

Martin Luther said the following about self control. Note how direct he is.

'Listen to the word of God which says keep sane and sober that it may not be said to you in vain. You must not be pigs. Neither do such things belong among Christians. Do not think you saved if you are a drunken pig day and night. Everyone should know that such a sin is contrary to his baptism and hinders his faith and salvation.'

So do not allow yourselves to be out of control emotionally or out of control mentally. Bring your mind and emotions under the control of the living God. Otherwise you will not be able to pray effectively.

That is not to say that Peter is against spiritual ecstasy or spiritual experiences when we pray. Such experiences are right and they affect our emotions. If your emotions are not affected from time to time, something is not right with your spiritual life. But your mind can be bypassed at the two extremes of human experience. Those who emphasise ecstasy in worship can easily bypass the mind so that in intercession they are not focused on what God demands and promises, they are simply having an emotional experience. At the other extreme, those who emphasise liturgy, with set prayers, also bypass the mind. If you consistently pray, week in and week out, the same prayer, the tendency is to do it by rote and not to think about what you are saying. So at both extremes there is a danger to abuse our minds.

When you come to God in prayer, it is essential that you be led by the Spirit of God and also be self controlled and sane, with your mind and emotions focused on the task of prayer.

So what is it you need in order to pray for the lost in your community? You need to remind yourselves that Christ died for the lost, but you also need to experience a burning concern for them, so that you will pray for them lovingly. There must be a combination of Word and Spirit. The Word informs our minds, and the Spirit energises our emotions.

God moves in response to prayer. I don't know why God chooses to do so, but the Lord of the universe has chosen to affect the world through answering the prayers of his people. God calls his people, both as individuals and churches, to be the means through which his power is released into the community in ever new ways. We must work and we must pray. That is why we must be clear minded and self controlled.

But above all, Christians are to 'love each other deeply, because love covers over a multitude of sins' (verse 8). Peter does not mean that the sins are covered over in a wrong sense. Rather, he means that love sees the sin clearly, but then covers over its consequences. Our faults are clear to some, but they are most clear to our families. Those of us who are married know that our spouses see our faults more clearly than anyone, but their love enables them to cover these faults from others, and also to continue affirming and caring and wanting to support us.

Interpersonal relationships in the church are constantly fraught with danger because the church is not simply a social club with a common aim or goal, it also has a spiritual dimension. Satan is not interested in disrupting things at the squash club, but he is interested in disrupting things in the church, and inevitably he will do everything he can to set people against each other. Such tactics are part of a Satanic plot, because when the church moves forward in unity and passion and power, the devil is afraid, his forces are thwarted, and his kingdom is driven back. So we must not be surprised when the devil tries to drive wedges between us as the people of God.

That's why love covers a multitude of sins. It does not mean that Christians look at each other through rose coloured spectacles, that is the difference between love and infatuation. Love is not infatuation. Biblical love is a deep seated, radical commitment to continue to love each other, despite all the obvious faults each of us clearly has.

Because each church is made up of a multiplicity of gifts, abilities, intellectual levels, cultural backgrounds, musical tastes, only fervent brotherly love will cover the multitude of sins and wrongs and personality defects and failures and weaknesses which will be there. Each church must be a community where each member has radical love for one another, where each will cover over a multitude of sins, and where each will help all the others to move on together.

Hospitality is a practical expression of this radical love: 'offer hospitality to one another without grumbling.' In the first century, providing hospitality for travelling preachers and other journeying Christians was an essential component of local church fellowship. Inns for people on journeys were dangerous for Christians, and that for two reasons. First, they tended to be brothels and so they were places of sexual danger. Secondly, they were places where travellers were often mugged and relieved of their finances. In other words, the places were physically dangerous and morally dangerous.

Church meetings in the first century were largely only attended by Christians. Non-Christians, interestingly enough, were not often encouraged to attend. Therefore, a common way to evangelise in the first century was to invite people into your home, for example, to a meal.

What we have we should use on behalf of others, giving hospitality in our homes and sharing our resources. This is very important in our postmodern world, where people are suspicious of all institutions and are particularly nervous of what happens in the church. Some of us have been Christians for such a long time that we have forgotten how terrifying it is for some non-Christians to come in a church door. Hospitality is not only something that builds up the people of God, it is an evangelistically potent force.

Peter also reminds the believers of the importance of the correct use of spiritual gifts: 'each one of us should use whatever gift he has received to serve others, faithfully administering God's grace in its various forms.' In every church there are gifts, natural and supernatural, and we should be putting them into practice for the benefit of the body. The word 'administration' was used in the first century for a steward serving in a home. He was responsible to make sure that everything that came into the household, such as food supplies and other commodities, was stored appropriately and ready to be served at the right time. So 'faithfully administering God's grace' means using our gifts and abilities in the church, and outside it, in ways which makes sure that God's purposes for our church work efficiently and well, and that the kingdom of God continues to go forward.

I like the following illustration which highlights the need for all the available gifts to be used. Each local church is like a bus; those who use their gifts are outside the bus pushing, trying to get the bus to its destination. Those who are not using their spiritual gifts are inside the bus, adding to the weight. They may be very enthusiastic, even knocking on the windows, and yelling encouragement to those who are outside. But ultimately the best thing for them to do is to get out and push with the others to increase the momentum of the bus.

Remember how Winston Churchill encouraged the country during the dark period of the Second

World War: 'On Friday evening last, I received from his Majesty the permission to form a new administration. In this crisis I think I may be pardoned if I do not address the House at any length today. I have said to this House, as I have said to the ministers who have joined this government, I have nothing to offer but blood and toil and tears and sweat. We have before us an ordeal of the most grievous kind. We have before us many months of struggle and suffering. Come then, let us go forward together with our united strength.'

Just as many people instinctively recognize Winston Churchill to be the author of these words, so believers should recognise God's voice when he speaks. To those who are involved in preaching, this is an awesome, incredible, overly heavy burden to bear. But it is a reminder that we must not trivialise what happens in the pulpit, or in our homes when we do small group work around God's Word. Those who speak must take cognisance of the fact that we do not simply churn out our own ideas in some random display of learning or even some form of human enthusiasm on a subject which happens to have gripped us. Rather we are to be so sensitive to divine help that what we give to the people of God as food is the very words of God himself.

Every Christian is not called to speak publicly for God, but each is called to serve God. And if anyone serves he should do so with the strength which God provides. As we use our gifts, we can draw on the resources of eternity by asking the living God to give us his strength and his power. God wants to enable us as we serve in our tiredness, in our weariness, in our disappointments.

But what is the goal of using spiritual gifts? It is that in all things God may be praised through Jesus Christ. How often leaders and other church workers can feel utterly unappreciated, utterly uncared for. They are desperate for a word of affirmation. But the thrilling thing is, that ultimately we are not serving God for human applause, but for the praise of God himself. We do it all so that Jesus may know praise and glory. That can be a tough lesson to learn, but it is fundamental to Christian maturity.

Then Peter gets so excited and bursts into an emotional expression of praise: 'To him be the glory and the power for ever and ever. Amen' This is the goal of our loving each other, of offering hospitality to each other, of using our gifts and abilities. It is that God may be honoured and glorified. The focus is not on us and our practical Christianity, but it is on the great, awesome Lord. I can almost imagine Peter dictating his words faster and faster. I can imagine Silas, the secretary, asking him to slow down.

14

More About Suffering
(1 Peter 4:12-19)

This section contains relatively little new information about suffering. After all Peter has written a whole letter dedicated to the theme of coping with suffering. It is a recurring refrain throughout the letter. Even so, there are several important details that will help us face difficult situations.

Dear friends, do not be surprised at the painful trial you are suffering, as though something strange were happening to you. But rejoice that you participate in the sufferings of Christ, so that you may be overjoyed when his glory is revealed. If you are insulted because of the name of Christ, you are blessed, for the Spirit of glory and of God rests on you. If you suffer, it should not be as a murderer or thief or any other kind of criminal, or even as a meddler. However, if you suffer as a Christian, do not be ashamed, but praise God that you bear that name. For it is time for judgement to begin with the family of God; and if it begins with us, what will the outcome be for those who do not obey the gospel of God and, 'If it is hard for the righteous to be saved, what will become of the ungodly and the sinner?' So then, those who suffer according to

God's will should commit themselves to their faithful Creator and continue to do good.

Verse 12 begins with 'Dear friends', a very common phrase in the New Testament meaning 'loved ones'. Peter is reminding his readers that he loves them. His letter is not an academic treatise about why there is suffering in the world. Rather, these are the words of a pastor to people in need.

Then he says, 'Don't be surprised at the painful trial you are suffering as though something strange were happening to you.' The word 'painful' is translated in some of the older translations as 'fiery'. 'Look,' says Peter, 'part and parcel of the Christian faith is the trial component.' The illustration Peter uses is the refining process that involves fire burning out all the impurities from a metal. In other words, being a Christian was not going to be easy. Peter is stressing what his Master had said years previously to his disciples: 'In the world you will have tribulation. But be of good cheer for I have overcome the world' (John 16:33). Jesus' expectation for his people is that they will face suffering.

One of the reasons that the church in this country is less involved in suffering than it might be is that our Christianity is often so domesticated, so lacking in radical application of the teachings of Jesus. Instead it is linked with the status quo, and so we are acceptable to our modern society.

One wonders, however, if we were the radical Christians that Jesus intended us to be, would be persecuted? In any case, I suspect that, within the next few decades, we may face a period of persecution, perhaps greater than we have had in the past. I don't know what form that will take. But Christians could easily be accused of intolerance because we believe that we have the truth. And that is to go against the current attitude of tolerance. The wind in our culture, the atmosphere in which we live, is in a direction which sees God as largely irrelevant. Inevitably, Christians are battling against the prevailing currents and moods and that is bound to mean buffeting and turbulence in our lives and a degree of persecution of one kind or another.

It is the opposition we face that causes some believers to backslide. They find the wind is a bit chill and it is hard work standing out for God in their place of work or in their family. Many have found that it is easier to stand still or move back. But God calls us not to face the winds in our own strength, but by the power of the Holy Spirit.

Suffering and glory
Verses 13 and 14 give a new perspective on suffering: 'rejoice that you participate in the sufferings of Christ so that you may be overjoyed when his glory is revealed.' Suffering and glory go together. In an incredible way God's glory is

triggered in the midst of suffering. There are many testimonies down the centuries of believers who in suffering saw far greater evidence of the glory of God than have Christians who never experienced any form of suffering.

There is here what theologians call an eschatological emphasis; eschatology means 'the last things'. In other words all suffering is to be seen in the glory dimension which is to come, in the wonderful realisation that each of our lives has its destiny in that point where there will be glory upon glory upon glory. It will be impossible to get away from this drenching in glory.

So what held Peter, among other things, was this vision of God's glory. When we are insulted for the name of Christ, we are blessed, for the Spirit of glory and of God rests on us (verse 14). Even though our suffering is relatively small, we go through it, not simply knowing that God's glory will be revealed through our suffering now, but in that future day of glory our sufferings of this moment will be nothing compared with the stupendous glory that will be given to us.

Wrong reasons for suffering
Having given a new perspective on suffering, Peter in verses 15 and 16 mentions the possibility of believers having to suffer, not for the sake of Christ, but because of their own sinful actions. This is a pertinent message for the Church of Jesus

today. Sometimes we suffer because we did an inappropriate action and we are continuing to suffer the consequences of that behaviour. We deserve to suffer from the state if we are guilty of criminal acts such as murder and theft. But I want to highlight the sin of being busybodies. The word is only used here in the New Testament, and some scholars think that Peter invented it. Literally it means 'those who look into things that are not their things', which literally is busybody or interferer. Meddling is not a criminal offence, but interfering busybodies are a tremendous pain in the life of the church. How much trouble is cause by gossiping! Therefore, don't be the sort of person who creates confusion and dissent in the church.

If you are going to be persecuted, be persecuted for being like Christ (verse 16). However if you suffer as a Christian, do not be ashamed, but praise God that you are being identified with the Christian faith.

God calls us not to be ashamed of our allegiance to Jesus. We are to wear our Christianity with pride, knowing that Jesus has changed our lives. And yet, at times, many of us have found it difficult not to be ashamed of being associated with Jesus. Even Peter himself had denied Jesus when his Master had been arrested. How thrilling to know that Peter received forgiveness – and the Peter who crumpled under

In this passage, Peter uses the word 'Christian' to describe believers. Nowadays we are used to the label, but it was not a common title to begin with. It was used initially in sneering contempt at Antioch. Before then, believers had been called disciples, or followers of The Way. But there in Antioch they were first called Christians – 'followers of that Christ'. Remember Agrippa's sneering put-down at the end of Paul's sermon: 'Do you think with such little effort you can persuade me to become a Christian?' i.e. 'a follower of this Christ'.

pressure in the courtyard was the same Peter who stood on the day of Pentecost before thousands and proclaimed his allegiance to the Son of God. What was the difference between the two Peters? It was the Spirit of God. How we need the Holy Spirit to give us confidence in being Christians.

Suffering and God's assessing our lives
In verse 17 Peter reminds the people of God that they will come under God's judgement: 'For it is time for judgement to begin with the family of God.' Judgement here does not mean condemnation, but to being weighed in God's balances. Christians are not only to receive God's blessing, in addition he will weigh their lives, and refine them through suffering.

So suffering sometimes is a matter of divine testing, it is a matter of the divine shaping of our lives. We need to be refined and shaped and changed. The attitude of the Church of Jesus should constantly be sitting in submission to the weighing of God. We should constantly be asking, 'Lord, we want to walk with you, we want our church life to reflect you in every area, be it in organisation and planning and strategy, or in worship and praise and prayer. Lord, weigh us!'

Response to suffering
If you are suffering for the right reasons, for living in the will of God, you are to do two things: (1) commit yourselves to a faithful Creator; and (2) continue to do good.

The word 'commit' is a banking phrase, literally meaning to place a deposit with a friend for safe keeping. What Peter is saying is that Christians are to entrust their lives to God, even when they do not understand why they are going through terrible sufferings. What we need in times of suffering is not an explanation of why suffering happens but the comfort of knowing the Creator. Often in pastoral care I find myself sitting with people in the most trying circumstances: a partner has died, a marriage has broken up, a massive catastrophe has happened. Often they will say to me, 'Why does God allow this?' I rarely answer that question, because what is needed at that point is not an explanation but the comfort of the living God. Explanations will be useful later on. But in the middle of suffering, most of us need not an explanation but the comfort of someone who loves us. Be assured that God loves you very much. He is your faithful Creator.

And 'continue to do good', not only because it is right, but also because it creates the habit of doing good. It is important to create the habit of doing good, so that when we do not feel like doing good, such as when we are suffering, we still go on doing good, and God is honoured and blessed. Many of us, when we are in suffering, stop doing good and retreat into our shells; we are angry with God, we are angry with the church, we are angry with everybody. But we are to do the right thing whether we feel like it or not.

15

Leadership
(1 Peter 5:1-7)

Peter, as we have seen, has written a letter to encourage believers to cope with suffering in such a way that they will live successfully in a dangerous world. And now Peter deals with the question of leadership in the context of suffering:

> To the elders among you, I appeal as a fellow-elder, a witness of Christ's sufferings and one who also will share in the glory to be revealed: Be shepherds of God's flock that is under your care, serving as overseers – not because you must, but because you are willing, as God wants you to be; not greedy for money, but eager to serve; not lording it over those entrusted to you, but being examples to the flock. And when the Chief Shepherd appears, you will receive the crown of glory that will never fade away.
>
> Young men, in the same way be submissive to those who are older. All of you, clothe yourselves with humility towards one another, because,
>
> 'God opposes the proud but gives grace to the humble.'
>
> Humble yourselves, therefore, under God's mighty hand, that he may lift you up in due time. Cast all your anxiety on him because he cares for you.

At times, when reading the New Testament, we are not sure what the word 'elder' means: does it mean elder as in the role of leadership in the church? Or does it mean an elder statesman, an older person, in the life of the church? This passage is such an occasion. Peter obviously refers to the role of leadership in verse 1, but in later verses he also refers to older people being involved with younger people in mutual submission.

Elders in church leadership need not be old but they do need to be mature. Eldership is not primarily a matter of age, but is a matter of gift and of spiritual maturity. It is clear from other passages of scripture that a church should not make a new convert, whatever his age, an elder.

In verse 1 Peter establishes his credentials to speak on the issue of leadership. Notice that he does not stress his apostleship but appeals to them as a fellow elder. Peter's style is not bombastic or dictatorial, he is open to other leaders and shows a humility towards them. Humility is the key characteristic of a church leader. Leaders have to give a strong lead obviously, but they have to be humble in their leadership – and it is to humble leadership that people will respond with humility. Peter models humility, he doesn't just talk about it.

Peter also describes himself as 'a witness of Christ's sufferings and one who will also share in the glory that is to be revealed'. Peter had seen not only the way that Jesus was treated by the authorities during his three years of public ministry, but also Peter saw his sufferings after he was arrested. But Peter also puts the suffering of leadership in the context of the glory which is to come. Anyone who emphasises any form of leadership has to know that there is a sense in which we are identifying with Christ's leadership style, which ultimately was that of a suffering servant. And anyone who wants to be a leader, but who has not grasped the motif of the suffering servant, cannot be the leader God wants them to be. Genuine, biblical leadership involves following in the footsteps of the suffering servant.

Leaders would be immensely crushed if they did not keep in mind the glory that is to come, to know that one day all the things that are said about them and to them, that they feel are unfair and hurtful, will one day be put right. Therefore my attitude as an elder in my church family is not to be defensive or negative about those who may seek to criticise or disagree in any way. It is to be involved in the listening process and to remind myself that one day all will be revealed; and if I was wrong, it will be pointed out to me; and if I was right I will find justification in God's glorious presence. Leaders have to throw themselves on God's mercy and look to the day when the glory will be revealed.

The elder's role is to be a shepherd of God's flock that is under his care. Shepherds were very common in ancient times, everyone had seen a shepherd walking ahead of his sheep. The shepherd really had two tasks: to lead the sheep to pasture and to tend the sheep. In the Middle East the ground is often barren and grass is rare, so shepherds have to lead the sheep from one place to another in order for them to get enough to eat. On the way the sheep may be damaged in some way, for example, brush up against a thorn which could inflict a nasty wound on the sheep. The shepherd's main task was the repair of the sheep and the providing of pasture for the sheep.

And that is the task for those who aspire to the role of eldership; they are called to feed and to tend believers. Leaders are to provide pasture so that the believers are fed, and to provide help when they are damaged. One of the most significant roles that eldership must do is that it must provide good food from God's Word. And if they are not providing

Peter is very aware of his pastoral responsibility. You will remember that classic encounter at the end of John's Gospel where Peter, who has denied Jesus three times, is re-instated three times. It is a wonderful, symbolic parallelism so that in the three denials, Peter is three times re-affirmed by God. 'Peter, do you love me?' 'Feed my Sheep'. 'Do you really love me?' 'Shepherd the flock' and so on. So the commissioning of Peter at the end of his life is to be a shepherd, and to provide pasture and to provide care.

this good food the believers will be ill fed.

Peter points out things true leaders will *willingly* avoid. No-one should recruit other people into the leadership task against their will. Leaders are to be willing to be involved in the service of God.

They are not *to be greedy for money*. Some elders, in the first century, earned their living from the collections that came from the people of God. But in the main, they were involved in an occupation. Nevertheless, some could be greedy for any extra finance that could come their way because of their role in the church. This is a huge challenge to leadership. They must watch their motivation.

Neither are they *to lord it over those entrusted to you*. There is a danger that people will become elders in the church and then feel incredibly proud of themselves and begin to lord it over the people of God. These leaders imagine they have a special right and place and privilege and so demand attention. The temptation in leadership is always to lead in the wrong way. There is always the temptation to assume power for its own sake. This is often where tensions arise in churches. So elders must be humble and gentle and open to criticism and rebuke and correction.

And leaders are *to avoid hypocrisy*. They must not say one thing and do another. There have been tragic examples of leaders who for years have preached sexual morality and their lives have been a lie. That is obviously hypocrisy of the grossest kind. But every leader faces the tremendous difficulty to live as well as he speaks. One of the great temptations of the preaching ministry is to preach better than one is living. To be an example to a congregation is the hardest thing possible.

In verse 4 there is a reminder to elders that they will receive the 'crown of glory': 'And when the Chief Shepherd appears [that is the shepherd to whom all the other shepherds, the elders, are responsible] you will receive the crown of glory that will never fade away.'

Everyone in leadership, whatever your role, elder of otherwise, is to work for the applause of heaven, not for the applause of men and women. That is what the crown of glory that will not fade means. This is the motivation for service. If your motivation is for people to appreciate you or you are seeking for human applause, your leadership will be short-lived.

Submission

In verses 5-7 Peter reminds his readers of the need for mutual submission. He first refers to those who are younger: 'Young men, in the same way be submissive to those who are older', but then immediately enlarges his application: 'All of you clothe yourselves with humility towards one another.'

Today submission is a thorny issue in the life of the church. And if leaders are constantly demanding submission from the people, it becomes brutalising, it becomes a huge disincentive to do anything. But if the people of God constantly refuse to be submissive, it becomes discouraging to the leadership because nothing is ever accomplished.

How often do we hear comments such as 'Who's in charge?' This kind of statement reveals a misunderstanding of the concept of servant leadership. Servant leadership is not weak leadership, it is not a mealy mouthed lack of knowing what God is saying. Rather it is a humble leadership, a listening leadership, a leadership which senses God, not only by the direct influence of the Holy Spirit, but in and among the people of God.

Unless the leadership is submissive to God and submissive, in one sense, to the people of God, and the people of God are mutually submissive to the leadership, the whole thing doesn't move as God wants it to. But where there is mutual honouring and humility then God moves among his people. Therefore 'clothe yourselves with humility'.

The term behind the English translation 'clothe' means a garment which has strings in which you tie a knot. Literally, the nearest garment we have is an apron. So Peter is saying, 'Apron yourself with humility.' I remember that each Sunday lunchtime, my grandmother would put on her apron and then make the food. To be 'apronned' is to be prepared for work. When you put on an apron you are not preparing for pompous entertaining; no, an apron is what you wear out of sight of the guests. This is the work clothing, not showing-off clothing.

Why is this important? Because God stands opposed to the proud but gives grace to the humble (verse 7). Pride is arrogance, and arrogance comes from a belief in yourself. Pride can be both obvious and inverted. Some of the most insidious forms of arrogance are actually very quiet, very hidden, very difficult to detect.

The opposite of pride is what the old translations call 'easy to be entreated'. Pride will kill godly leadership as it will kill godly followership. For such assert for themselves a position that only Jesus may fill. In the leadership of the church and in the life of the church, we have to hold many things tentatively for we cannot be certain what the right thing is. But we do it because we are following Jesus. Sometimes leaders have to say, 'We think this is the right thing to do and we want you to move ahead in this particular way', but all the time they are keeping an ear out to what Jesus may say. Only Jesus is infallible. So it is with humility that they exercise leadership in whatever sphere, and it is with humility that the church exercises followership in whatever sphere. Do not strive for position. Do not pushing forward for public acclaim or support. Do not want promotion or attention in the church. Instead humble yourselves under God's mighty hand and in due time he will lift you up.

Whoever you are in this leadership dimension, there is a place of refuge for you when things get tough: Cast all your anxiety on God because he cares for you. The picture here is of a soldier coming in at the end of a journey carrying the equivalent of a big rucksack, and as he came in through the door exhausted from a long walk, he took off his burden. Some Roman officers would have servants to take off their armour. They would lift it off the shoulders and place it in a place of storage. That is the concept here: cast off your burdens, take off all that weight, by letting God care for you. He comes to removes your burdens, that is how much he loves you.

16

Resist the Devil

(1 Peter 5:8-11)

Be self-controlled and alert. Your enemy the devil prowls around like a roaring lion looking for someone to devour. Resist him, standing firm in the faith, because you know that your brothers throughout the world are undergoing the same kind of sufferings.

And the God of all grace, who called you to his eternal glory in Christ, after you have suffered a little while, will himself restore you and make you strong, firm and steadfast. To him be the power for ever and ever. Amen.

The first letter of Peter comes to its conclusion with a reference to the devil. Now the devil has had a mixed press in the course of the twentieth century. There has been continuing ridicule of a personal devil. So during most of the century, Satan was seen as very much a figure of fun. Even in evangelical Christianity, the big enemy was the world. Believers were encouraged not to be worldly, in the senses of not smoking cigarettes, drinking alcohol, or going to the cinema. But in the 1980s the emphasis of both the world and the church turned to the activity of Satan. Many films such as *The Exorcist* were concerned with the para-normal. Demon possession became common talk among both Christians and non-Christians.

Peter has a very helpful emphasis for us in terms of the devil. Although we are to be aware of his activity, the focus for the life of believers is not to be on the devil but on Jesus, the victor over the evil one.

How to resist the devil

Because of the activity of the devil, believers are to 'be self controlled and alert' (verse 8). To be self-controlled literally means 'don't be out of control' and, as we saw earlier in the letter, it is a word taken from intoxication. But it means to be self-controlled in every situation. Be in control of yourself; don't let your temper or the circumstances or anything dictate how you behave. Be in control of your life. When you are not, it is a great opportunity for Satan to be at work. To be alert means to stay awake. Just as when you are driving your car your eyes droop from tiredness, you respond by forcing them open. Look around and be aware of all that is going on.

Now the test for the believer is to stay alert and self controlled, not in the crises but in the humdrum of our lives. Both verbs – 'be self–controlled' and 'be alert' – are in the present continuous tense. Peter is reminding believers that the Christian life is a marathon and not a sprint.

We need to stay awake for the long haul. One danger facing Christians is that Satan is often more patient than they are. Sometimes mature Christians are more in danger from the devil's activities than new Christians because they fail to retain a state of red alert in their lives.

Why do we need to be alert in this way? Because our enemy is literally our adversary. It is a word taken from the courtroom. The prosecuting counsel, the one who accuses us, is the devil who prowls around like a roaring lion, looking for someone to devour. One of the dangers for which shepherds had to be on guard was lions who would be looking for easy prey. The word 'devour' literally means 'to gulp down', to swallow in one bite. Satan, like a lion, looks round the sheep fold, looking for a stray believer to pounce on. That is why we need to be self controlled and alert.

But if our focus is constantly looking around to see where Satan is, then we will become obsessed with evil and we will find it everywhere. The best thing for a sheep to do was not to go wandering around the edge of the flock looking to see if the lions were near, but instead to stay close to the shepherd. So often in church life, people get obsessed with the devil and attempt to confronting him everywhere. This kind of spiritual warfare makes us negative and destructive as we begin to be absorbed in the personality and the characteristics of the evil one. Remember that although Satan is dangerous he is a defeated foe. He may be a lion, but he is a mortally wounded lion. Stay close to the Shepherd and you have nothing to fear.

Let's face it, these early Christians needed this reminder from Peter. They lived in a world where the demon forces were constantly worshipped through various gods and idols. The demonic was much more obvious than it is for us in the western world at present. But, as you know, for many Christians working overseas, the demonic is very real, and much more like a first century setting.

So there is an enemy to resist. Peter tells his readers to 'go on resisting him by standing firm in your faith' (verse 9). Don't allow the devil to get his own way. Don't let him have influence in your life. Go on resisting him until the day you die and go to be with God.

Persistence is a very important mark of Christian maturity, yet sadly it is a much neglected spiritual attribute. In the Christian Church there have always been those who have risen to a certain degree of fame with meteoric speed but who in a few years are nowhere in the service of God. In the church we should honour those who walk with the Lord through all of their lives, who go on resisting the evil one.

Notice the commitment to *the faith*. We are to stand firm in the truth. Stand firm in what you know to be true. There is going to be an increasing pressure on us as evangelical Christians to compromise what we believe. But we are to stand firm on the historic revelation of God. Do not be pushed aside from the whole council of God. We have an enemy to resist and we do so on the basis of the faith revealed in the Bible.

Encouragements for resisting the devil
We are also helped in standing firm by the example of fellow Christians: 'because you know that your brothers throughout the world are undergoing the same kind of sufferings.' We are not on our own. There is something tremendously encouraging about knowing that we are not being singled out for suffering. All over the world where Jesus is preached and proclaimed, his disciples come into contact with alien forces which oppose both them and the message of Jesus.

It is so releasing and encouraging to realise that others are going through the same problems and difficulties that we are facing. Often in the pastoral situation people will come and share with me their need or burden. Sometimes I say to them, 'Do you know that a number of others have also said that to me?' And it is so reassuring for them to be informed of this. One of the worst feelings is to be alone in suffering. But no-one who suffers for Jesus is alone in his suffering.

Despite having to suffer, we have a secure future because God is the God of all grace (verse

10). Grace is getting something we do not deserve, when God pours his love out on us. Why does he do so when we do not deserve it? He does it because his heart is toward us.

Not only will he give us grace for every situation, he has also 'called you to his eternal glory in Christ'. What a future destiny to have! Eternal glory. So in the middle of all your suffering, remember that when God called you to new birth, he gave you his birthday card on which was written his promise of future glory. In your suffering remember that you will have this eternal glory which is never going to disappear.

Throughout his letter Peter has developed an interesting link between theology and doxology (the Greek word *doxa* means 'glory'). Good teaching about God leads not to academic sterility but to doxology. Good theology, rightly taught, always leads to praising God. So Peter comes to the conclusion of his letter by pointing a way to the glory of God, not as some abstract thing, but as something in us from the day we believed – his eternal glory given to us in Christ.

Peter promises his readers that four things will happen despite their suffering: God will restore them, God will make them strong, God will make them firm, and God will make them steadfast.

'Restoration' seems to be taken from the medical profession and the last three words are taken from the building profession. These last three ideas of being strong, firm and steadfast are almost mirror images of each other. I am not sure what the difference between them is. The word 'restore', however, is the same word used in Ephesians 4 where Paul writes about apostles, prophets, evangelists, pastors and teachers whose task is to 'equip' the saints, or to 'repair' the saints. What God will do for us when we have been through a period of suffering is to repair us and to restore us. It is a word used of a splint, placed around a broken bone to keep the bone in place to enable it to grow back straight. So Jesus will restore you, he will make you whole again.

And he will make you – in the metaphors from the building trade of being strong, firm and steadfast – firm foundationed. You will be built on solid rock. At the moment in your suffering you may feel that you are living in an earthquake zone and everything is insecure under your feet. You don't know whether you dare take a step forward because things are falling apart all around you. After a little while Jesus will put your feet on a firm foundation, so that you will be secure where you tread. For some it will occur in this life. For others the complete fulfilment of that restorative healing, the complete fulfilment of that rock certainty, will be deferred until we are together with God experiencing his full glory with him forever. But it is a wonderful promise and we are to live now in the light of it.

Jesus is Lord

'To him be the power for ever and ever. Amen' is a wonderful response to God. Interestingly the word for 'power' is a classic political statement. The power source in the ancient world was Rome, with Caesar dominating the whole culture of the day. But where does power lie for these poor people that Peter is writing to? It is not the Roman authorities who are persecuting them. The ultimate power in the universe is God. This power resides in Jesus forever. By implication Peter is saying to his readers, 'One day, Caesar will be dead. One day the Roman Empire will dissolve.' All earthly institutions are temporal by their very nature. All human exercises of power are flawed and ultimately doomed to failure. But Jesus reigns forever. And that is why we put our trust him.

To our Jesus be power for ever and ever.